Acclaim for

Love the Kid You Get. Get the Kid You Love

David Altshuler has been urging us to "Put the Child First" for the almost forty years that I've known and worked with him. He has helped many youngsters (including my son) find their own best path towards healthy growth and individuation. I've referred him many of my adolescent patients and their parents, and have consistently found them most satisfied—the best tribute to his wisdom and expertise.

David's weekly blog has always been a delightful mixture of wry humor and timeless insight into that most important and most difficult thing we strive to do well—raising our children. I invite everyone to experience this excellent compilation of his perspectives on parenting and life.

Thomas O. Bonner, Ph.D., ABPP
President, Dade County Psychological Association

In a world in which for many parents, every test is a competition, every school activity a resume-builder, and every moment of recreation a wasted opportunity, David lends his much-needed voice of reason to the dialogue. His writings encourage even the best parents and mentors to cast a critical eye on their approach toward those in their care, and like a master teacher, he leads you down a path by which you can't help but take a fresh look at those things you might have thought were settled parts of your repertoire. David has something to offer everyone, and his anecdotal — and at times tragically funny — approach, along with his masterful observations of the human condition, not only make for an enjoyable read but an essential one. David's work should be required reading for anyone who raises or works with children in today's overscheduled, hypercompetitive, and increasingly shrinking world.

Gregory Cooper, J.D.
Ransom Everglades School

i

As a developmental psychologist who specializes in prevention and intervention research with adolescents, I am acutely aware of the complex challenges they face. I have known David Altshuler for years and his commitment to youth is unparalleled. His perspectives are thought provoking and insightful. David's use of real life anecdotes to convey vital advice and guidance is not only creative, but extremely accessible. His second book has an even greater focus on familial warmth and connection across generations. It is reminiscent of the long historical tradition of tribal cultures where elders would gather with younger generations and share their wisdom through stories. This new book is a definite contribution to the field and a must read for anyone working with teens.

Michelle M. Hospital, Ph.D., L.M.H.C.

David Altshuler's clever anecdotes, realistic advice, and professional experience as a father, a consultant and an educator, fosters the culture needed to raise healthy kids. David shares the rewards of parenting through focusing on loving our children and building relationships with them. Children know how much they are loved and accepted when time is spent with them in activities that interest them. David's ability to provide thoughtful opportunities for parents and educators to laugh at ourselves in our quest to love our kids is applauded.

Kim Stephens, Dean of Enrollment, Wasatch Academy

Love the Kid You Get. Get the Kid You Love picks up where Raising Healthy Kids in an Unhealthy World left off. While these essays are darker, the advice is even more gentle and more actionable. This book is a must read for every parent, therapist, consultant, and mental health professional who cares about normally achieving children and those with emotional, cognitive, or behavioral challenges.

Bruce Turkel

David and I have worked collaboratively on cases for many years so we are friends as well as colleagues. We both understand the challenges parents face raising children today. David has a wealth of experience, knowledge and insight into the minefields that parents and kids walk through. He is able to guide us in a sincere, empathetic and humorous way, while challenging us to consider our parenting strategies. In his latest book, David offers us another opportunity to benefit from his professional expertise and his experience as a parent, so we can make sense of the constantly changing attitudes and values in our society. His storytelling allows readers to examine their own attitudes and beliefs about parenting in a world that seems to have been turned upside down. David's use of humor and his non-threatening style make this an easy read for any parent or professional who wants to learn some practical ways to encourage healthy decision. We raise children in a landscape that constantly asks us to bend and conform to ideals that are often contrary to the best interest of our children. All parents can benefit from this book. David is a thoughtful, wise and sensitive and cares deeply about families. This book will help us connect with our children, be better parents, and continue to challenge our own best thinking. I highly recommend this book to parents, professionals and anyone who interacts with children!

Raymond S. Estefania, MS, LMHC, CAP, CIP, ICADC
Co-Founder and Executive Director, Family Recovery Specialists
Addiction Professional and Therapeutic Consultant

I love this book! I just wanted to read the whole thing in one sitting, devouring it page by page, story by story. David is one of those rare individuals who can actually see the forest for the trees....he can look at a complex situation and cut straight through it, condense it to a much simpler way of understanding, infuse the situation with some great wit and wisdom, and then, all of the sudden, the complex situation isn't actually so complex after all. It's crystal clear. This is why I love to read everything that David writes, and why, as a fellow educational consultant with a similar practice, I keep David on speed dial for when I can no longer see the forest for the trees. Using his 30 years of experience as an educational consultant, David brings professionalism, insight, perspective, experience, and an unparalleled sense of humor to the biggest challenges parents face. I suggest you get your copy of his newest book delivered as quickly as possible—may I suggest that new same-day drone delivery?

Rebecca Grappo, M.Ed., C.E.P., founder of RNG International
Educational Consultants

This is not a book to be read once and then put on a shelf; rather, it is a wealth of information to be referenced as the journey of parenting unfolds. In his second book, David raises essential parenting questions, and through rich storytelling, readers gain strategies and insights to promote positive development in young people. Parents will benefit from David's passion and advice, but not just parents -- anyone who works with young people as they navigate adolescence and transition into adulthood will find much wisdom here. Over the years I have had the privilege of listening to and learning from David's stories, and it is exciting to know that now you can too!

Adam Rainer, MBA
Shortridge Academy, Founder and Executive Director

I have the perspective of living next door to David. Because I live in "a world of words" in my day job, I am fortunate to have observed David Alshuler in his "real life". He cares about adults, too, but his priorities are clearly focused on kids. Indeed, his actions speak louder than his words, in his day-to-day care for his own children and those of other parents, and children living in our neighborhood and communities elsewhere. So, in what little time I have to spare as a single parent, I read his books.

Dominique Musselman, M.D.

"David writes like he speaks. There are serious messages in these stories that he uses to teach, and he does not pull his punches when discussing some piece of destructive or self-defeating behavior by a kid or by an adult. But his message is intelligent and educated, and clearly based on extensive personal and professional experience. David handles the problems and dilemmas of childhood, adulthood, and parenthood with a light touch, so he is never preachy or moralistic. Rather, David follows his own advice to readers--he is clear and direct with others, he believes in setting limits on his own and others' behavior, but he does it with the compassion and warmth of someone who understands human foibles. Recommended reading for every human being on the planet."

Andrew Lagomasino, Psy.D., Clinical Psychologist

Thank You David, for your help and guidance in providing us with a working toolset of knowledge. You have again produced a book that everyone will find easy to read. Even the time pressed parent will undoubtedly not find it forbidding or cumbersome. Your book embodies what makes families work, and identifies what can be detrimental to the success of the family system. Raising healthy and responsible kids is the most challenging, deeply spiritual and complex undertaking in the life of every parent. An undertaking that is besieged by unhealthy distractions and influences in today's society. Here is a book that assists us to navigate this crucial task. It is loaded with valuable, sensitive guidelines for parents, professionals and anyone who invests in raising children with lifelong positive values.

Aneisha Samuels, M.S.,C.A.P,

Psychotherapist and Addictions Specialist, Miami Children's Hospital.

During a checkup the other day a lovely mother glanced at her three children and looked me in the eye and said, "The days are long, but the years fly. As a pediatrician and mother of three, I was struck by her words. Similarly, David Altshuler's book <u>Love the Kid You Get. Get the Kid You Love</u> stops you in your tracks as it shouts out truth. It made me chuckle one minute and become teary eyed the next. David's cleverly described vignettes depict nuggets of truth wrapped in wit and humor. In a world filled with anxiety and uncertainty, David's solid timeless wisdom is greatly needed. His years of clinical experience and knowledge have given him insight which is both remarkable and practical. Consider his book a must read for anyone interested in bettering themselves or helping a child.

Kaylee Kuhn, M.D.

Love the Kid You Get.
Get the Kid You Love.

David Altshuler, M.S.

Langley Press

To my beloved children

Table of Contents

Introduction

If these essays are as much fun for you to read as they were for me to write, I will be pleased. If they are of benefit to you and your family, I will be honored.

Your comments are always welcome. You may connect with our on-line community at DavidAltshuler.com

I can be reached directly at David@Altshulerfamily.com

Where is Your One Hundred Foot Long, Shimmering, White, Gleaming, Metal Something?

Flamingo, in the heart of the Everglades, is 38 miles past the ranger station that welcomes natives and tourists alike to the National Park. There is a bait and tackle shop with sandwiches, ice, and souvenirs on the spit of land—emphasis on the word "spit"—that juts out into Biscayne Bay. Hardly a garden spot to begin with, Flamingo has never recovered from when Hurricane Andrew smacked it back into the Pleistocene 20-something years ago. Most folks fill up their gas tanks and head out into the bay in their motor boats, but, there are canoe rentals as well.

A two-hour paddle can bring a father and son to a point pretty squarely in the proverbial middle of nowhere. The nearest city is back the way we came: past the Snickers Bars and bottled water, up the 38 miles to the ranger station, through Homestead, and back to "town" such as it is. Noticing that the tepid water was now down to about 18 inches, "town" was the direction in which I was most interested because—stop me if I mentioned this before—there was nothing where we were and significantly more nothing in every direction. Getting stuck in the muck under the brackish water wasn't an option because in the Everglades stuck is stuck. Waiting for the tide to come in is what's happening because getting out and walking isn't. Everglades muck isn't quicksand, but it'll do.

So I had almost convinced my son to agree to turn the canoe around when, maybe a half mile to the north, on a spot where the land hit the water, we spotted an impossibly long, possibly metal, glimmering, shiny, white something. It was hard to tell, squinting into the sun, but whatever it was seemed to be about 100 feet long.

"What's that?" my son asked.

Having dodged questions of this type—"Why is the sky blue?" "How much do hippopotamus ears weigh?"—for some years, I felt confident in responding, "Beats the heck outa me." And then after a pause for thoughtful reflection I added, "It can't be a space ship."

My son lifted his paddle out of the bay and listened to the water lapping against the side of the canoe. "Well, if it's not a space ship, what is it?" We continued to stare cross-eyed into the distance. "Let's go see."

As ideas go, "Let's go see" is right up there with "Let's invade Poland." Maybe it looks good on paper, but there isn't—lacking air support—any practical way to go about it. "You can't get there from here" is nowhere more true than in a foot and a half of water. But my son was already out of the canoe and dragging the craft and his dad out of the bay onto what could charitably be called "land".

Or trying to.

Because he was immediately ensconced in muck up to his ankles.

He took a step, or tried to, and lost his sandal in the muck. (Neither one of us had brought running shoes as we had not planning on doing much jogging in the canoe.) Quickly determining that returning to my house with a muck-covered son would be easier to explain to my wife than coming home without the boy at all, I followed. And was immediately knee deep in muck. Our every labored step now produced exactly the kind of slurping and squishing noise the existence of which polite people are trained to ignore. It took us ten minutes to crawl a hundred yards. But we could make out the shimmering, white, gleaming metal something much more clearly now.

It was definitely not a space ship.

Another ten minutes and another hundred yards closer and stuck in the muck up to our hips, it occurred to me that, should an eight-foot alligator happen to wander by, we would look like yummy people-kabobs at a reptile bar mitzvah. We would be unable to defend ourselves—alligators are notoriously undeterred by rubber footwear—and would be chomped. Our lower halves would be left undisturbed under the muck, a silent warning should anyone else in subsequent generations brave this desolate mucky place.

I kept the notion of eight-foot reptiles wearing yarmulkes to myself, but did suggest turning back.

"But what do you think it is, Dad?" My son replied. "And we've come this far."

I could not argue. We were now over an hour on the clock and a quarter mile through the muck from the canoe. The shimmering, white, gleaming metal something was getting bigger in our vision. Clearly, it was more than a hundred yards wide, pure white, maybe two-feet high. But what it was we still couldn't guess. It couldn't be man-made. There were no men here to make it; there had never been men here, and there never would be men here. We were in muck-ville. No one had ever lived or would ever live here. Clearly, an advertisement for Burma-Shave was out of the question. We were not looking at an abandoned bill board nor did a rocket ship seem any more plausible.

Our situation seemed like a bad riddle: "What's a hundred yards wide, pure white, and glimmers on top of the muck?"

So we kept crawling laboriously on all fours so as not to sink irretrievably into the mud and looking into the horizon. About a quarter mile from the shimmering, white, gleaming metal something, we were able to discern that there was a strip of brown on the hundred yard wide strip of shining incandescent white. The brown stripe was now distinguishable from the background of stumpy mangrove trees that littered the murky swamp.

At a hundred yards away, we stopped again. The crawling, tedious to begin with, had now crossed the border into downright unpleasant. Impossibly, the shimmering, white, gleaming metal something appeared to be vibrating. In the middle of the expansive swamp, where there could not possibly be life, there was life.

And then the shimmering, white, gleaming metal something came apart, separating into a thousand component pieces as white pelicans took off at the same instant exploding up into the horizon in every direction.

Which brings me—"finally" you might say—to my point about parenting: You have to be in it to win it.

The concept of "quality time" is, in my judgment, complete and utter bullshit. Parenting is about "real time." You can't go up to someone whom you hardly know and talk about relationships, reproductive biology, and physical intimacy. A stranger in the street isn't interested in your values, ethics, and insights into how to live a good life. Why would your children value these aspects of who you are unless you have laid a foundation for communication by spending some no-agenda time together?

Here's the question: What is YOUR shimmering, white, gleaming metal something? You don't have to go out with your kids into the muck 38 miles past the ranger station. In fact, come to think of it, I'm not sure I recommend any activity that potentially sets you up as reptile stew. Your shimmering, white, gleaming metal something can be found closer to home: in your garden, in your kitchen as you refine your recipe for cranberry muffins, in the wood shop in your basement building a rocking chair, or in your garage repairing a motorcycle. Where ever you hang out with your kids will do. Of course, I would argue that your shimmering, white, gleaming metal something is probably not going to be found in a clothing store in the mall or on a glowing screen, but I don't pretend to know everything.

Here's some gentle, directed advice: this weekend, put down the glowing rectangles and forget about homework. Instead, just take the kids somewhere and do something.

You never know what you might find glimmering on the horizon.

Happy, Happy, Joy, Joy!

Sixteen year-old Paula is unhappy at her rehabilitation facility in California.

She was happier last year before ending up in treatment. She was happy when she was running away from home, getting into cars with strange adult men, staying away for days at a time, binge drinking, and using IV drugs.

Paula has been making some slow progress in treatment. OK, let's be more honest: she's barely making any progress at all in treatment. She doesn't "get it," that drugs were destroying her life, that her future outside of treatment was time limited, that the issue was not "if" but "when" something truly terrible happened. (By this high standard of truly terrible, her STD doesn't even make the list.)

Still, where there's life there's hope and where there's sobriety—even enforced and unwelcome sobriety—nothing truly terrible happens in a given day. Paula may not be making significant strides therapeutically, but she's not popping Oxycontin with vodka chasers either. At least she's not waking up next to who knows whom after having done who knows what.

Paula's treatment team and I agree: Paula is a severe substance abuser, probably an addict. She's different from many folks, those for whom an occasional drink is a pleasure not an issue. Some people can even drink a six pack of beer and not have a problem with alcohol. Paula is not one of those people. I feel strongly that if Paula drinks, Paula will die. Stated unequivocally, as a direct and foreseeable result of her drinking and drugging, Paula will die an early, preventable, and tragic death. I'm not much for making predictions but unless Paula commits to sobriety, I doubt she'll see her 25th birthday.

Paula has complained to her parents back in Virginia that she isn't making any progress in treatment. And, she says, the school at the treatment center is even worse. The chemistry class is too hard and the English class is too easy. Some of the other girls on the cross country team don't take running seriously enough and other girls take the sport too seriously.

Paula's parents are furious with me. In our weekly phone calls, they point out Paula's lack of progress; they blame me for recommending this expensive facility; they speak, at length, about how insensitive Paula's chemistry teacher is and how incompetent her English teacher is. They tell me how, were Paula not in treatment, she would likely be running 5K in under 24 minutes instead of her current best time of 25:20.

Paula's parents are agreed that yes, perhaps, Paula needs to cut down on her alcohol use and that, indeed, she probably shouldn't use illegal drugs for a while, but why am I insisting that Paula can't ever drink again, that she can't even have a glass of champagne at her wedding? Why am I so mean? Why can't Paula have her old life back minus the drugs and alcohol? Why does she need to be in treatment if treatment isn't working? Why won't I recommend that she come home to be with her loving parents who miss her terribly, who only want what's best for her, who just want to spend time with her?

My argument is that every day that Paula is sober, she learns another way to get through the day without using. I admit that she's not making great progress internalizing her other issues; it's true she still has trouble regulating her mood and that her eating disorder isn't getting any better; it's true that she's not learning much chemistry and that her English class may be too easy. My point that at least she's alive, seems not to resonate with her parents. Paula's parents want her to be happy. They are going to pull her out of treatment and bring her home.

Imagine staring at an object on the horizon. You are unable to discern any detail on the ship; it's just too far for you to see clearly. The more you try to focus, the more obscured the distant vessel becomes. Finally, you glance away, and look a few degrees to one side. As unlikely as it sounds, you are now able to see the ship more clearly—even though you've stopped trying to see it directly.

Nothing is harder that seeing our beloved children unhappy. But focusing on our children's happiness is the least effective way to allow them to find contentment and fulfillment. Indeed, happiness is a hard deer to hunt.

Which child is more likely to be happier? One child is given a huge home complete with finished granite counter tops in the kitchen, immaculate walk-in closets, and a polished marble staircase. The other child is given the tools and materials to build his own home. In addition, this second child is told by his father that they will work together to build the house although the project will probably take a couple of years and will require significant hard work and sacrifice. It is likely, that over the course of the project, the father and son may drop tools on their feet, argue, and use inappropriate language.

If you agree that the first child—the one who is given a perfect home—will be happier, do you also agree that Paula's parents should take her home so that she will be happier?

If you agree that the second child—the one who will take time to work with his dad on building the home—will ultimately be more content, do you also agree that there may be some unhappiness and frustration during the construction project?

And that it's okay for our kids not to be happy on a given day?

3

Tenth Grade Math

One of my running buddies is, by any objective measure, absurdly successful. He is blissfully happy in his personal life with a supportive, accomplished, well-spoken wife. They are that rare couple who met young, fell hopelessly in love, have been happily married forever, and now have three adolescent children whom they adore. Professionally, Ben is the CEO of a company with over a hundred stores across the country. As a boss, he is capable, thoughtful, and insightful. Ben's employees worship him; his board of directors likes him; his competitors admire him. He has wicked business skills—he can read a balance sheet from across the room; he knows when to open a new store and when to close one; he has enough knowledge and information to sense incipient trends in his industry before they happen.

For all of Ben's abilities there is one glaring deficit: he can't do tenth grade math.

I'm not saying that Ben is in some way deficient because he can't do tenth grade math. I'm not being condescending in that I, the Great David Altshuler, CAN do tenth grade math. To the contrary, I am suggesting that Ben doesn't need to know tenth grade math. How can you argue that if he did know tenth grade math he would be better off in any way?

For example, would you have the unmitigated temerity to suggest that Ben would have TWO HUNDRED stores across the country if he knew tenth grade math?

I didn't think so.

***

I chatted recently with one of my old colleagues, a science teacher. I acknowledged that under no circumstances could I pass the first quiz from the first week of his tenth grade chemistry class. My buddy cheerfully admitted that he could not get many questions right on a test that I gave when I taught tenth grade math.

Yes, I have a graduate degree; no, I am not smarter than an tenth grader. There's nothing wrong with our school curriculum. But there's nothing divinely inspired about it either.

Ben and his family were over at the house the other Saturday and I watched his middle son play Parcheesi with another family friend also in the tenth grade. It was clear from their playing that neither child had the first clue about simple probability. Ben's son didn't position his pieces at the ideal striking distance to capture his opponent's pawns. I felt about this the same way that you might feel about a young man who took his life savings out of the bank in cash and walked down Flagler Street throwing hundred dollar bills in the air shouting, "Come back to me, Mama Hundreds!" However, having read my own columns about keeping my mouth shut, I said nothing to the young men huddled over the Parcheesi board. They seemed to enjoy themselves pretty well. They were obviously content to go through their 16-year-old lives oblivious to my great insights about probabilities and strategy in Parcheesi.

Competence in core subjects in critical. I don't see how people could get through the day without fifth grade math—the ability to add and subtract and make budgets, for example. Excellence in your desired field is critical.

You have to know all there is to know about your profession. Otherwise you won't be competent or successful. Knowing as much as you can about as many different topics is a bonus. All educated people pride themselves about their understanding of disparate topics.

But not every successful, contented person has to know math at the tenth grade level.

Maybe Ben is so accomplished not in spite of the fact that he doesn't know tenth grade math, but because he doesn't. Maybe Ben is able to take appropriate risks where I sit back over-analyzing with the Expected Value Theorem. (The EVT helps measure risk and reward. I use the EVT to play Parcheesi. Maybe that's why I can usually beat Ben's kids.) Maybe Ben's skill set—eloquence, business savvy, charisma, risk taking—are exactly those abilities that aren't taught in tenth grade math.

Maybe those skills—the most critical components of Ben's success—aren't taught in school at all.

Remember that quote about law school? "The A students become law professors; the B students become judges; the C students become wealthy attorneys."

What's the message here? Am I advocating for mediocrity and ignorance? Of course not. A little knowledge is always good and a lot of knowledge is always better. But next time your son comes home with a C in tenth grade math, consider whether or not he has the skills to marry the woman of his dreams, have three adorable children, and be the CEO of a successful chain of a hundred stores.

Then take out the Parcheesi board and have some fun. If your kid learns enough probability to have a solid grounding for an undergraduate statistics course, that's good too. But don't believe for a minute that tenth grade math skills are the only ones necessary for success.

Trouble in Paradise

Sometimes it seems that the stars align and I get just the information I need just when I need it.

Stated another way, when the student is ready, the teacher appears.

I've been having some trouble with my heroes lately. It turns out that one of the people whom I greatly admired is not just a cheater and a liar, but also a bully. And if intimidating his fellow athletes wasn't enough, it turns out that rather than fessing up to his misdeeds, he "doubled down" each time the authorities were on his tail; he coerced his team mates to tell lies as well.

I loved this guy, trusted him and believed in him. Before I found out what a psycho he is. Admittedly, I was naive, but I just could not accept the evidence before it was conclusive. Besides, he looked us in the eye and told us that he was clean.

Before this guy's fall to disgrace, another of my running buddies had seven pictures of him on his wall. Rather than medical degrees, my friend had photos of our mutual hero. Why didn't my buddy have "board certified this" and "diplomat" that on his wall? "Because," he explained. "Anybody can go to medical school."

Needless to say, those photos have all come down.

Basically, this guy whom I looked up to for years, destroyed an entire sport— a sport that had been and should have continued to be filled with honorable, bighearted folks—with his blatant fabrications, his viscous enforcement of "omerta," and his quasi-psychotic insistence that he hadn't done anything wrong—"never failed a drug test"—as he so offensively put it.

Worst of all? Think of the first "clean" rider. Maybe he finished 23rd. Heck, maybe the first guy not using needles, hopped up on EPO, finished 123rd. Think of that guy who trained hard and trained fair his whole life only to finish repeatedly at the back of the pack because he was one of the few who didn't cheat.

My ex-hero is responsible for that travesty as well.

***

Then this biography comes out about another one of my heroes—a rock star not a bicyclist. And it turns out that this guy too has his imperfections. He has been mean to women, thought about firing his band members, and been insensitive to employees over the years.

I was stuck and sad. These are the two guys I had always thought about meeting—maybe going for a run, having a BBQ in my backyard, introducing their kids to my kids. In short, my heroes.

Not anymore. I didn't want anything to do with either one of them. Until another one of my running buddies explained it all to me around Mile 10 last Saturday. "First of all, there's a difference between these two men," she began.

"One was living a vicious lie and destroying the lives or his team mates. That's unforgivable. Any good that this fraud may have done is erased by his disgusting disregard for any semblance of truth and by his threats to the livelihoods of his fellow riders." I nodded my head in agreement. "The other guy just had a few bad moments. Basically a decent man, he had a biographer comb through his 67 years. Of course the writer was able to dig up a few imperfections. That's a big distinction—an entire career built on fraud versus a basically good man committing a few indiscretions along the way."

And here's where the teacher appeared and brought the narratives together: "If you picked the five worst things that I've done in my life," she said. "My bio wouldn't read all that well either."

Well said. And more than fair.

***

As parents, we have to try to make the right call all of the time. But we also have to acknowledge that sometimes—hopefully on the smaller issues—we are going to fall short. Consistency is the issue.

If we model appropriate behavior, our kids will be more likely to do the same. If we make the occasional mistake and forgive ourselves, our kids will come to understand that it's okay to fall short sometimes. And when they make a mistake, they'll be able to own up to it and keep going.

Without resorting to lying, cheating, and bullying to cover their tracks. Without breaking the hearts of the people who have admired them for years.

5

We're Number One! We're Number One!

There is nothing more important than my child being Number One. It's not about skills; it's about place value. Unfortunately, I've been going about the business of making my child Number One all wrong. Fortunately, I now know what to do to ensure that my child is Number One from now on.

Previously, to ensure that my child was Number One, I helped her by making sure she was studying constantly and by doing her homework for her. When the homework got too difficult and time consuming for me, I hired tutors to do her homework and write her papers. I also had to make sure that my child understood the work so that she could do well on exams. When my child would try to fall asleep after five or six hours of studying with her tutors, I would poke her and slap her to keep her alert and attentive. Of course, I also prepared her snacks high in carbohydrates to keep her focused. When these foods didn't work efficiently, I gave my child amphetamines and an intravenous glucose solution.

All these interventions worked well enough—my child has A grades in all her classes—but there was a problem. There was another child who also had A grades in all her classes. My child was Number One but this other child was also Number One.

Worse, the children were friends, playing together on weekends and wanting to have a "sleepover" whatever that is. A sleepover? No, thank you. Out of the question.

My child refused to compete with her friend. "We both have A grades, Mommy," my child said. "She is my friend. I don't want to beat her. We can both be Number One."

What nonsense. I tried to explain to my daughter that, mathematically, there is only one Number One. How could there be two of the same number? In order for my child to be Number One, everyone else's child must be some other number. Number Two, for example.

That's when I got the good idea. Since there is nothing more to do to help my child be Number One, I am going to help this other child be Number Two.

If this other child's parents were to get divorced, for example, this other child would be upset and unable to focus on her studies. Therefore I have taken a handkerchief from the mother's drawer and placed it at the home of a neighbor—a bachelor. (I got this idea from a play that one of my child's tutors was reading to her, "Othello," I think it was called.)

Now, I won't have to pay so much money to tutors to keep my child as Number One. Maybe, I'll even be able to take the IV needle out of her arm. Most importantly, my child will now be Number One all by herself.

Helping this other child to be Number Two by having her parents get divorced is such a good idea. I don't know why I didn't think of it years ago.

***

At the risk of "explaining the joke," here's why this mom is in the running for the "Worst Mom of 2014" award: she's teaching her kid to be dishonest; she's teaching her kid to care only about being Number One; she's teaching her kid not to care about learning; she's teaching her kid not to care about friends.

She's also attempting to commit an unconscionable act. As those of us who have read "Othello" (or had "Othello" read to us), will remember, it ends badly.

The shift from inspiring your child to be Number One by "helping" her learn to inspiring your child to be Number One by harming her classmates is not as big a jump as it might first appear. The more I think about it, the more blurry the distinction becomes. Helping your child to cheat and harming another child may have similar motivations and similar outcomes. Of course, there's a difference. I'm just not sure it's a significant difference. If the intent of helping your child is the same as the intent of harming her classmates, then the message, "It's about winning" is all that our children will hear.

As more and more parents focus on their child being Number One rather than on helping their child acquire skills to the best of her ability, the more reprehensible behavior we're going to see.

You heard it here first.

You Don't Say

Following is a gentle guide to help you determine when it is appropriate to make a comment and when it might be better to keep your thoughts to yourself.

1) "Teachers should be compensated based on the test scores of their students."

You get to remark about compensation for teachers only if you have taught in an overcrowded classroom of recent immigrants with limited English proficiency. If you put in 180 days with 35 children in a classroom built for 22; if you were able to help those students overcome the fact that there are few books in their homes nor quiet places to study; if you have dealt with children with un-diagnosed learning differences in the same class with children with attentional issues; if you facilitated high test scores for these children yourself, then you get to comment.

If, on the other hand, the closest you have come to a school is remembering what it was like to go to one many years ago, then you get to hush.

2) "People should speak English."

You get to say this if you speak another language fluently, a language that you learned as an adult, a language that you learned while working 40 hours a week, a language that you learned without instruction.

3) "People should get jobs."

You get to say this if you yourself, as a recently downsized adult worker, found a job in a difficult economy.

4) "He should have caught that."

You get to say this if you yourself, as a professional athlete playing the sport at the same level, have made that catch.

5) "People should get off drugs."

You get to say this if you yourself have overcome chemical dependency, if you know first-hand the craving that comes with addiction, if you yourself have gotten through a day wanting nothing more than to use drugs or alcohol.

6) "Children with learning differences should do well in school."

You get to say this if you yourself have compensated for learning differences and been successful as a student.

Otherwise, you get to hush up.

Interestingly enough, those who HAVE taught in difficult circumstances and been successful; those who HAVE learned a foreign language as adults; those who HAVE found jobs in a difficult economy; those who HAVE made that tough catch; those who HAVE kicked addictions; those who HAVE achieved despite learning differences...

...are the last to insist that others should be able to do the same. Indeed, the best teachers are those who know how hard it is for some students to learn some subjects. My colleagues in the field of addiction who are themselves in recovery are the most understanding of those who lapse.

As in so many things, a little graciousness goes a long way. Going forward, I am going to endeavor to be less judgmental and a little more understanding. I hope you'll join me.

What Can You Do?

Dr. Coleman hit the ground like a sack of potatoes and did not move. An instant before, he had been doing well enough—to my untrained eye—in the fighting portion of his brown belt test, but now he lay inertly on the floor of the ballet studio that served—on Tuesday and Thursday nights—as a dojo. I was tempted to go to Dr. Coleman's aid, but there were actual medical professionals in the class of a dozen students watching the "kumite," so I remained sitting uncomfortable on my ankles.

After a few seconds, our teacher looked up from his notes. Motioning to one of the other doctors in the class—our group seemed to be weighted heavily with health care professionals—he asked, "Is he dead?"

"No, Sensei."

"Then move him out of the way."

***

Contrast the above scene with the following—admittedly brutally insensitive—joke: A mother is carrying her 12 year-old son from a limousine to the door of a five-star hotel. "What a shame he can't walk," says the doorman."

"With any luck, he'll never have to," the mother replies.

***

As with all parenting issues, moderation is the answer. Throwing a child in a lake is an abusive form of swimming lessons. But the other end of the continuum, not allowing a child the opportunity to help out around the house, is equally harmful.

Admittedly, it is unlikely that your adolescent children WANT to help out around the house. Did I say that I thought your adolescent children wanted to help out around the house? Is there any sentence is these hundred articles I've written on parenting that would lead you to infer that I am a deranged alien with no knowledge of how children are raised on this planet? (This is a rhetorical question to which the correct answer is "no.")

Adolescent children don't want to take out the garbage, do the dishes, mow the lawn, vacuum the floors, bathe the dog, or—if they are lucky enough to live in a home with a pool—clean the pool. The tricky bit is to allow them to want to help out, to find the middle path. Because the "evil dojo method"— "sweep the floor or you don't get any food" is as bad as the "we carry him everywhere so he doesn't have to walk" School of Parenting. Kids who are carried are never allowed to do any chores. And why would they?

As always, preparing the soil has much to do with growing healthy plants. It is extraordinarily difficult for an adolescent to disengage from playing "Shoot, Shoot, Shoot, Blood, Blood, Blood, Kill, Kill, Kill" to come help prepare dinner. If there are no addictive screens in the home—and need I remind you that all screens are addictive?—then helping to set the table becomes a more palatable activity. It is hard for parents, indeed it is hard for any flesh and blood creature, to compete with those dopamine inducing video games. But we can eliminate the competition. There is only one way to beat a video game: unplug it.

The other way to allow children to participate in the gentle interactions that contribute to the running of a productive home is to take the time to encourage them to do so. Remember, the goal isn't just about getting the brownies made. We're working on hanging out with the kids, accomplishing a shared goal, maybe learning some math (if three teaspoons is one tablespoons, how many teaspoons is two tablespoons?) If the goal was just getting brownies, you could drive to the store, take $3.95 out of your wallet, and buy some.

Let me know what gentle persuasions work in your home. In the meantime, I'm going to see whether or not Dr. Coleman has regained consciousness.

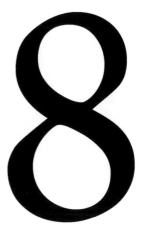

How Could Anybody Be So Stupid?

Think back to the last time you heard a Really Loud Noise.

Was the Really Loud Noise a truck backfiring? How far is the nearest road? Could a sound have traveled that distance? Is it the Fourth of July? New Year's Eve? Could the Really Loud Noise have been a fire cracker? Was the Really Loud Noise a gun shot? Where are the children? Are they indoors? Are the children safe?

All these thoughts—trucks, holidays, fireworks, guns, children—went through your head in a split second. But split that split second into many parts and here's what happened way before all those thoughts sprinted through your awareness: your body reacted. Before you had started to analyze what the Really Loud Noise was or whether or not the Really Loud

Noise actually represented danger, you were startled; your heart rate went up; your senses were heightened, you started to breath faster.

In other words, there is a part of your brain than responds before language. There is a part of your brain that responds before conscious awareness.

Which shouldn't be too surprising. There are all kinds of bodily processes going on that aren't processed. Run around a track and your body responds beautifully. There are systems in place that allow you to run fast, but not too fast. You are unlikely to be able to force yourself to run so fast that you die. And let's not even talk about all the swallowing, spitting, blinking, and sneezing that goes on without your being aware. Your neocortex, the "thinking part" of your brain is what separates you from your less evolved ancestors, but your neocortex isn't the whole show. Your limbic system, your "reptile brain," shows up for work every day also.

Which brings us—"finally" you might say—to the topic this week, addictions great and small.

Samantha is doing beautifully on her diet. Over the course of six months she has lost 26 pounds, exercising five days a week and eating sensible meals. Her sense of herself is at an all-time high. She is wearing new outfits and meeting new men.

Yet on a Thursday night instead of going to bed at 10 o'clock so that she can wake up early the next morning to get to the gym, she somehow finds herself in the car heading to Farm Stores to devour a half gallon of chocolate chip ice cream.

Ray brings the crops into town, crops that he and his three sons have labored in the Alabama sun for months to produce. After selling everything, Ray has enough money in his pocket to pay the mortgage and support his family through the winter. Ray goes into a bar "for one quick drink" before driving the team back home.

Two days later, Ray emerges back into the sunshine, wondering what happened to the previous 48 hours and all the money. He has no recollection of having had all those subsequent drinks nor of having any fun. As a result of his poor judgment, his family loses the farm. Ray's children and grandchildren have to work on land owned by other people.

Haley has kicked her reliance on cocaine and been clean for a full year. She is scheduled to appear in court tomorrow where a thoughtful judge will undoubtedly expunge the charges against her and allow her to regain custody of her children who have been in foster care. All Haley has to do is remain sober for one more day to get her life back on track. Needless to say, Haley chooses that day to relapse. As a result, she is incarcerated. She never sees her children again.

Mickey has an undergraduate degree in mathematics and has worked professionally as an accountant for 20 years. He advises his clients about risk and reward and counsels them about long term investment strategies. Yet for all his knowledge about index funds, he goes twice a year to Las Vegas where he plays slot machines and blows every dollar he has earned in the previous six months. At almost 50 years of age, he has no savings for retirement. His children will not be able to afford to attend college. After threatening to do so repeatedly over the years, his wife finally leaves him.

How could anyone be so stupid? How could any rational person use such poor judgment, engage in such self-destructive behavior, act without any regard to future consequences? Samantha's blown diet, Ray's drunken binge, Haley's ruined recovery, Mickey's degrading obsession—what are these people thinking?

The answer is in the question. These decisions aren't sensible. These decisions are driven by a part of the brain that is, by definition, not rational. Before you judge an addict, before you deride the stupid decisions, before you throw up your hands in disgust, before you throw a stone, ask yourself if you have ever known craving, if you have ever taken a step in the shoes of someone who has.

Or as Eric Clapton said, "Before you accuse me, take a look at yourself."

Craving—the kind of craving that only be described to non-addicts through the metaphor of "hunger"—lives at a level below reason, below consciousness. Telling addicts to use their higher order cognitive abilities to think about the future consequences of their behaviors is like telling yourself not to be startled the next time you hear a Really Loud Noise.

Up a Tree without a Paddle

Look! Up in the Tree! It's a Bird! It's a Plane! It's a... It's a Child?

On the Stanford Early School Achievement Test appeared the following question: five year-old students were shown three pictures, a kitten in a tree, a snake in a tree, and a child in a tree. The children were asked, "Which of the these would cause you to call 911"?

Sandra, mother of an adorable five-year-old posed this question to our running buddies over breakfast one early morning last week. You may wish to take some time to consider whether a kitten in a tree, a snake in a tree, or a child in a tree would compel you to call 911 before reading ahead. Take all the time you need. I'll wait right here.

Ready? Put your pencils down. Our discussion begins with my buddy, Tim, a man of rare discernment honed over 30 years as a professional fire fighter. Tim felt strongly that the kitten in the tree was the correct answer. "That's what people always call us for, a cat in a tree" he said. Scratching his head he went on, "Of course, sometimes we wished they wouldn't. If we have actual fires to put out, for example."

Yet Tim was mistaken-sadly mistaken. Grossly mistaken. Horribly mistaken. Here he was, a college graduate with over a hundred men under his command, yet he was no smarter than a first grader.

Feeling equal parts sorry for Tim—poor thudpucker—and certain of the validity of her insight, Lorna spoke up next. "I see a snake in a tree I am calling 911 before you can say, 'Oh, shit! Look at that snake in the tree!'"

Sandra shook her head again.

And a hush fell over the assembled sweaty breakfasters.

Because products of Miami public schools that many of us are, even we could tell that if a kitten in a tree is the wrong answer and the snake in the tree is the wrong answer then the child in the tree must be the right answer. After a stunned silence, Tim spoke. "So, it's come to this. Children are supposed to suckle on screens, stay indoors in front of the TV. A child in a tree is wrong." Tim paused. "I'm glad my kids are grown," he said.

Standardized tests don't harm children; wrong answers do.

Where did we go so very wrong? Can it possibly be the case that a child in a tree is now so unlikely as to merit an emergency call? It is probably just as well that 911, which was first used in 1968 but did not become well known until the 70s, was not around when I was a kid. To the best of my recollection, my friends and I lived almost exclusively in trees exiting infrequently to forage for sandwiches or find more rotting boards to bring up into said trees to build what could charitably have been called "forts" but were in actuality a collection of surfaces with bent and broken nails sticking out of them at dangerous angles. When we got tired of the trees we would walk down to the bay and swim out to the barrier islands to look for sea urchins. Sometimes we would find broken beer bottles, sometimes we would get tetanus shots. That we never actually drowned when swimming back from what is now an island covered with multi-story condominiums is a poor argument for allowing 12 year-old kids to play unattended. But there is something to be said for going outdoors in an unstructured way.

What do your kids do when you're not around? Is their every moment accounted for? After soccer practice do they go to piano practice?

Have you, as loving parents, scheduled a little boredom for the kids? If necessity is the mother of invention then a lazy afternoon outdoors might be the answer to many of our children's questions. For example, I'll give you odds that, left to their own devices, your children could come up with more sensible test questions that the ones currently found on the Stanford Early School Achievement Test.

10

Did I Say that Out Loud?

April showers will bring college admissions decisions and although "fat envelopes"—filled with roommate selection, immunization and myriad other forms—have been replaced by lengthy emails with links, the elation and sadness remain constant across generations. Thin envelopes still represent "we had too many qualified applicants." Fat envelopes remain the door to a world of possibilities.

Also unchanged is the tendency for second semester seniors to pay less attention to their studies. These kids have been admitted to college. Why would they study? Are you kidding? The only reason these kids ever learned anything in the first place was so they could get a good grade so they could go to college. You don't put a dollar in a coke machine because you want to watch the sun set. It's commerce.*

Here however is a note of gentle warning to those who have been accepted to college and are slumping like the 1951 Brooklyn Dodgers who lost their 13.5

game lead and then a three-game series against the Giants in which Bobby Thompson's home run—"the shot heard round the world"—is the greatest comeback of all time if you're a Giants fan but the saddest moment in the history of sport if you—or more accurately your grandparents—were rooting for the Trolley Dodgers: your acceptances are provisional. That's right. There's no free lunch and there's no guarantee that your space is the incoming class is reserved. If your 3.9 cumulative un-weighted grade point average becomes a 2.9, your first choice college can become a "woulda coulda shoulda" in a New York minute.

How else might you shoot yourself in the foot using a machine gun? Consider the following: Use your twitter feed to brag about your inappropriate behavior with alcohol. "After my interview at North Cornstalk College, I urinated on the statue of the president."

These 140 characters spell doom for the unsuspecting 17-year-old.

In a gentler age, the response from the college might have been more reasoned. As recently as 1993, a wonderful liberal arts college in Pennsylvania phrased their concerns as follows: "As I am sure you are aware, your performance during [the second semester] represents a significant decline from that of previous semesters."

Rut ro!

The letter went on to say, "Consequently, the Admissions Committee has determined that your enrollment status at [college whose name you would recognize] be suspended pending further review…" The accepted/rejected student was given the opportunity to do penance, to read some books and write some essays. The hope was that the "yes letter" would grow back.

In the days before "e"-stantaneous communication, it took longer for colleges to learn about a senior's grade of "D" in second semester calculus. An evening of poor judgment could remain a secret between the student and a puddle of beer barf in the woods. Now that students have access to decidedly un-social social media, colleges have instant access to whatever your seniors choose to expose. Just as an email is more like a post card than a letter, a tweet is shouted from the rooftops.

Admissions officers don't want to be the one who made the mistake and admitted the vomiting first year. It costs money to pay the lawyers who write the "you can't be a student here anymore" letters. Students who smoke pot and aren't even smart enough to keep the information to themselves are a strain on scarce college resources.

The more serious issue, of course, is not whether or not your poor judgment is public, but whether or not your bad choices exist in the first place. The point of this column is certainly not to encourage students to keep their indiscretions discrete.

But in the meantime, don't think colleges aren't listening to whether or not you're proclaiming yourself to be a twittering buffoon. Because they most certainly are.

* For the chronically irony impaired, let me state unequivocally: I am desperately in favor of learning for its own sake. Students who study only for grades bring dishonor to themselves and their institutions. Teachers who only teach to the test are no better.

11

The Only Thing Worse than Your Unbearable Mother-In-Law

At the height of the potato famine in January of 1852 in Ireland, a young mother addresses her husband. "We have little food and less money. Our son, our only child, is not yet two months old; he is hungry, as are you and I. There is barely enough food for the three of us. We cannot afford to have your father live here anymore. You must take him to the poor house."

Her husband says that he cannot leave his elderly and infirm father at the poor house, that the poor house is a euphemism for starvation, disease, and death. "Yes, times are tough," he says, "but where there is life, there is hope." The husband points out that they are a family, albeit a poor one and that what happens to one is what happens to all.

The wife persists. "Take your father to the poor house," she insists. "The food that your father eats is food that we could give to our son."

The argument persists for some weeks until, finally, on a bitterly cold and particularly hungry day, the father relents and agrees to take his father to the poor house. "Come on, Da," he says. "We have to go."

"I'm glad you've finally seen that this is our only choice," says the wife. "Here. We have a blanket in the closet. Take it and wrap up your father for it is brutally cold and the journey is long."

At this point, the baby speaks to his father. (That's right. The baby, who is only two months old, speaks.) The baby says, "Before you go, cut the blanket in half. Take my grandfather to the poor house to starve and die with only half the blanket. Leave the other half of the blanket here in the closet. For when it is my turn to take you to the poor house a generation from now, I will wrap you in the remaining half of the blanket."

The mother—shocked and chastised by her talking two month old—relents. The grandfather lives out the remainder of his days in the home of his son, daughter-in-law and grandchild.

The family lives happily, if hungrily, ever after.*

***

Let me begin by stipulating that your mother-in-law is unbearable. I acknowledge that no one gets along with her, not even her own family. I appreciate what a completely and utterly overbearing woman she is. You don't have to tell me; I'm convinced.

I'll be specific: your mother-in-law gives unwelcome, unhelpful, and inaccurate advice about how to bring up your children. Her insights, such as they are, might have been helpful in the mid-18th century in Eastern Europe but have no possible relevance today. Indeed, rather than antibiotics and modern medical science, her home remedies seem to involve castor oil on a good day and occasionally to require eye of newt.

Worst of all, her anxiety is off the charts, completely unbearable. I acknowledge, for the record, that just the other day when you wanted to take the kids to the park, your mother-in-law threw herself across the doorway of your home, slobbering incoherently about how the forecast called for snow, hail, and a plague of locusts of Biblical proportions yet you live in Miami where, to any objective observer, the weather seemed "pretty nice out."

Or as Ernie K-Doe of the Coasters sang in 1961:

She thinks her advice is a contribution
If she would leave that would be the solution

Before pontificating about what to do with your spouse's mom—remember
murder for hire is still frowned upon by legal authorities in many of our
United States—and how your children will be better off as result of said
profound advice, let me remind my gracious readers that Churchill defined
democracy as "the worst form of government on the planet. Except for all the
others."

Putting up with your mother-in-law is unbearable. I agree. You may not
remember, but I've met your mother-in-law. For no reason whatsoever, she
tried to run me over with her truck. I don't like her either. But the sad fact is
that you have to put up with her, call her, go over for a visit, pretend to like
that tasteless slop she shockingly refers to as "home cooked food."
Because the alternative, cutting her out of the life of her grandchildren, is
worse.

Model for your kids that even people who disagree can have a civil meal
together. Allow your children to understand that even people who have little
in common can make it through an evening without coming to blows. Show
your kids how much family means in your family.

In short, leave the blanket in the closet. Because the only thing worse than
your unbearable mother-in-law is a talking two month old.

* I would be grateful to any gentle reader who could point me to the origin of
this tale as I would like to give credit to the author.

12

Rejected from Amherst, Percy Goes to Live in a Trailer Park with an Older Woman and her Three Children then Gets a Tattoo

College admissions counselors are taught to communicate that "Admissions is a match to be made, not a game to be won." We are trained to help parents understand that a child who is academically and socially well suited to a university is more likely to succeed there than one who doesn't fit.

Consider John, whose senior year course work includes algebra II, English, and government, none of which is at the advanced level. His electives include "Rock Music," "Evolution of the Corduroy Suit," "Weight Training," and "Office Aid," ("Thank you for contacting Schmendrick High; how may I direct your call?") His grade point average is a low B, his test results about the national average. He has no significant extracurricular activities, participation in sports, or leadership. In his spare time he enjoys watching movies and playing video games. His recommendations, like his essays, are unexceptional.

If John were to be admitted to Amherst—he won't be; mortgage the farm—he would not be predicted to be successful in the classroom where the overwhelming majority of his peers will have gotten top marks in advanced placement courses throughout high school. Most first year Amherst students have already successfully completed a year of calculus before going to Massachusetts. What math course will John take with only a background in algebra II? There are no courses at Amherst in which he can thrive. There are no other courses in any departments for which he has the requisite background and skills.

John's failure to be graduated from a "top" college is not what is holding him back from subsequently achieving a PhD in philosophy from Princeton. John's path diverged much earlier. That John can't do well at Amherst is the sticky bit. It's not that he can't get it; it's that he can't get out.

Consider another student, this one who does have the course work, the background, the profile to be admitted to Amherst. But isn't. Percy has five advanced placement courses as a senior, is captain and leading scorer on the lacrosse team, has 97th percentile SAT scores. His essays and his recommendations are both brilliant.

Here's what never happens: Percy is rejected from Amherst and, as a result, doesn't go to a four year college at all. Instead, he enrolls at the local community college, studies automotive repair, is unable to handle the curriculum, and flunks out. After drinking wine in the gutter for a number of years, he moves into a trailer with an older woman and her three children.

And then he gets a tattoo.

Oh, for goodness gracious sakes. You know what happens to Percy when he gets rejected from Amherst?

He goes to Colby. And then he goes to law school.

And lives happily—or as happily as he would have had he matriculated at Amherst—ever after.
Colby is one of our country's great liberal arts colleges. In close to 30 years of practice, I've never sent a student there who ended up anything but blissfully happy. Maybe the average SAT scores of Amherst kids are marginally higher than those of the Colby kids. Whatever. If Percy has the profile to be

admitted to Amherst and gets an unlucky roll of the dice—it happens—then he has the ability to be successful elsewhere. He goes to Colby and studies his butt off and learns a bunch and goes to grad school.

Unless of course Percy believes in "Amherst or Die." In which case, he won't go to Colby. He'll sit around feeling wronged. He'll say "what was the point of all that studying? Why did I take all those advanced placement courses? I have to go to Colby. Oh, the horror." Here is a man who marries for money rather than for love. Here's a man who doesn't understand the joy of competition, who won't play unless he knows he can win. Hyper-focused on the future, he is unable to enjoy now.

In which case he has deeper issues—problems that Amherst is not close to capable of addressing.

As always, it's not the dog in the fight, it's the fight in the dog. Kids with skill in and out of the classroom do well long term. Kids without ability have issues that are independent of their placement. The expression, "No matter where you go, there you are" is true of our psychological baggage as well as where our children end up going to college.

What's the take away for loving parents who want what is best for their children? Focus on <u>who</u> your kids are, not <u>where</u> your kids are. Help your children acquire the skills that will allow them to be successful should they be admitted to Amherst.

Because cream does rise to the top. Even if, as frequently occurs, Amherst happens to choose a different container.

13

What I Like About You

What year were you married? What year was the baby born?"

"We were married in 1987, Abuela. Jacob was born in 1991."

MariaPaula's grandmother had started to show signs of mild dementia something over a year before and had recently moved in with her only granddaughter. As grandmother's cognitive abilities continued to slide, she asked "What year were you married? What year was the baby born?" more and more frequently. By the last year of her life, she would ask "What year were you married? What year was the baby born?" several times in the same hour. Robert and MariaPaula always offered the same patient, truthful answer. They had been married for three and a half years when Jacob joined them.

Robert and MariaPaula weren't offended. They saw no need whatsoever to point out that, although Jake hadn't been born out of wedlock, they had indeed moved in with one another several months before their marriage. It went without saying that grandma would not have benefited from that information. Nor did they point out that in modern day Scandinavia, the vast majority of marriages are to couples who already have a child. They understood that grandma was from a different generation and a different culture. "It was a great scandal back in Cuba for a woman to have a baby the same year you got married," MariaPaula had explained to her North American husband. "People might say that you had sex with your husband before you got married."

"Yeah, I get that," Robert had responded.

No amount of reassurance could ease abuella's obsession over the year of her granddaughter's marriage and the year of her great-grandchild's birth. Nothing else seemed to bother her. She clearly loved and accepted Robert. That he was from a different country, a different culture, and a different religion made no impact. And she adored Jake although, of course, at 22 he had been graduated from college and hadn't lived at home for some years. It wasn't until grandma died that Robert and MariaPaula understood the reason for her obsession with the year of their marriage and the year of their baby's birth.

An elderly relative explained: "Your grandmother had a child when she was 16. Of course, she wasn't married. The baby was put up for adoption and she never saw him again."

The issue was from grandmother's past, not from MariaPaula's. Abuella had had a child out of wedlock in a time and a country when such a circumstance was unspeakable though hardly unheard of.

The shame of that act and the sense of loss had followed her for over 70 years. When she could not remember the names of her children and grandchildren, when she could not remember the names of the days of the week, when she could not remember to get out of bed to go to the bathroom, she still remembered to ask, "What year did you get married? What year was the baby born?"

***

Ibsen communicated how the sins of the fathers are visited upon the children. Are you projecting "your stuff" on your kids? Are you concerned for your children or are you concerned that your children will be like you? When you say, "Do your homework" are you focused on your kids learning something or are you remembering how little you liked to study? When you give your kids advice about going forward in their own lives, are you in actuality thinking backward about your own?

The good news is that your kids are not you any more than MariaPaula's grandmother is MariaPaula. If you'll let them, your kids can grow up without the same anxieties that may have held you back.

If you let them.

14

Woof! Woof! Woof! Homework! Woof! Woof! Woof!

Our three year-old terrier mix is committed to ridding the world of evil squirrels.

When Langley sees a squirrel in a tree, our gracious pooch transforms into a psychotic lunatic. He sprints around the base of the squirrel-laden palms yelping frenetically. He leaps into the air, hurling himself upward in a deranged frenzy. With steel springs in his legs and infinite energy, he has a 40-inch vertical leap.

Of course, the trees—with the squirrels at the top—are 40 feet high.

What does our Langley expect? What is going on in his doggie brain? Does our 35-pounds of man's best friend think that the squirrel is going to exclaim, "Oh, I know. Here's a good idea. Let me scamper down this tree, so my furry corpus can be shredded and devoured by that hysterical, slavering idiot of a dog"?

Needless to say, the squirrel chooses a more discrete course and remains safely ensconced in the canopy; Langley continues boinging in all directions at once, barking incessantly, a dog seemingly high on an unfortunate cocktail of performance enhancing drugs and methamphetamine.

Contrast Langley's snarling and snapping with the following monologue: "Do you have any homework? Don't tell me you don't have any homework! I know you have homework! I went on-line to find your homework! You have Wordly Wise homework! You have Algebra homework! Why aren't you doing your homework? I've told you a hundred times to do your homework!"

Is there, by any chance, an analogy here between the concerned parent and my bounding canine? Do you find yourself screaming like a schizophrenic preacher on a daily basis for your kids to put down that @#$%^&*! phone and do their *&^%$#@! homework? Do you pontificate endlessly about how homework is necessary, how homework builds character, how homework is helpful, how homework is meaningful for the future, how homework must be done N-O-W?

Do you have more in common with my brown dog than might first appear?

Because if, as a consequence of your virulent spewing of words on the subject, your children actually DID their homework in a productive way (your children doing homework in a productive way would be analogous to the squirrel coming down from the tree,) it could be argued that there was method to your verbiage.

But if, no matter how long or how loudly you scream, the kids are only fulfilling their academic responsibilities in the most cursory was (the squirrel staying up in the tree) then it might be time to rethink your approach. Indeed, I don't think Langley wants any part of instant shredded squirrel stew. He has to be aware that he's never caught a squirrel before and that he's not going to catch one now. He benefits from his bounding behavior in other ways. He gets valuable exercise; he gets to be in touch with his inner-wolf; he gets to impress us with how muy macho he is.

Are there benefits of your yelling at your kids to do their homework?
1) Are you trying to communicate to your children that, in a perfect world, you would prefer that they be the kinds of kids who enjoy doing homework?

2) Are you trying to communicate that homework has some value?

3) Are you trying to communicate that you have given over the responsibility of educating your children to strangers who are overworked, underpaid, and subject to silly restrictions on how they can teach?

Here are my modest insights into each of the above:

1) Love your children for who they are, not for what they do.

2) The research is against you here. The younger the children, the more contra-indicated is homework.

3) Elementary school teachers are great. But your child is going to have to live with the consequences of his education more than her teachers will.

If by yelling at your kids to do homework, you are communicating that you have anxiety or that you feel there is something fundamentally flawed about your kids, then I have a palm tree you may wish to run around.

But you might want to consider that barking and leaping have never gotten Langley any closer to a squirrel.

15

Same Life, Different Day

"Satire is a sort of glass, wherein beholders do generally discover everybody's face but their own."

Jonathan Swift, 1667-1745

Norma is lovely. My wife and Norma have been friends since college. Norma went on to law school some thirty years ago and was subsequently appointed to the federal bench by Bill Clinton. My wife and I ran into Norma at the supermarket this week. Norma is so busy trying heavy duty drug cases that we don't see her as much as we'd like. In fact it had been several years since we had had a chance to catch up.

"What happened with that handsome guy you were dating?" my wife asked. Apparently not too many polite preliminaries are necessary between old college buddies.

"He turned out to be such a narcissist." Norma sighed. "We broke up over two years ago."

"He was a partner at that international business firm" my wife said.

"But what an ego. And selfish? You can't imagine."

"So are you seeing anybody?"

"Yeah. I started going out with this guy from work. He's a prosecutor in another division." My wife's eyes lit up, happy for her old friend. "But it's not going to last. He's so stuck on himself. And he's stressed over work, has no time for me."

"Has he met your boys?"

"Yeah, maybe I shouldn't have introduced them. But you know how it is. If you wait until you're sure the relationship is going forward before you let the guy meet the kids, you never have any time with the guy because you're always with the kids. But if you introduce the guy before you're sure the relationship is going forward, the kids think you're dating an endless series of guys." My wife nodded knowingly. Norma went on. "But he had no interest in my sons and not much interest in me either."

"Hey, speaking of the boys, how's your ex?"

Norma sighed. "Still the same old narcissistic asshole as ever. He sees the kids maybe four days a month. If that. They're 11 and 14 now. They need their dad."

"Let me guess," my wife said. "He's still only focused on his career. Same as it ever was."

"You got it. He never had time for me, always bringing work home, working all weekend, worrying about the next trial. He does make good money though, maybe five times what I do as a judge." Norma paused then added wistfully, "Not that he isn't four months behind on his child support."

"Do you ever wonder if maybe you should have stayed in private practice? You were as smart as your ex. You could be making that money."

"But who would take care of the boys? As a judge I can be home for dinner. As a trial attorney at that firm I'd be putting in the 70 hour work weeks too." Norma thought for a minute. "My children need one parent," she said. "Even if I can never seem to meet the right guy, I know that much."

My wife and Norma chatted a little more then hugged and cried and promised to keep in better touch. But as soon as we had loaded the groceries into the car, my wife lit in to Norma with both feet. "She so doesn't get it," she began. "It's been the same since she was 19-years-old!"

"What has?" I asked.

"Can't you see it? It's as plain as day. All those guys she's been dating, her ex-husband…"

"What about them? They seem like highly successful, accomplished guys."

"That's just it," my wife said exasperated. "They're always the same guy!"

I pulled over to the side of the road. That's how struck I was by my wife's insight. She went on.

"She always dates somebody she meets at work. He's always on a career track. Obviously, he's some high powered attorney. He never has time for her; he never has any interest in her boys. Her ex-husband was the same. This recent guy was the same. Heck, I remember the guys she dated in college."

My wife, never one to miss an opportunity for dramatic effect, paused. "He was the same guy too."

So now the bigger question becomes, who is going to bell the cat? Should my wife tell Norma that she always dates the same guy? Should she go on to say that the proverbial definition of insanity is repeating the same behavior and expecting a different result? Should my wife tell Norma up front that SHE OUGHT TO CONSIDER DATING GUYS WHO AREN'T HIGH POWERED ATTORNEYS BECAUSE IT JUST ISN'T WORKING OUT FOR HER?

Maybe Norma should get involved with a guy who teaches school. Or a social worker might be nice. Or a nurse. Or even an attorney who works normal hours.

But not these same high powered, crazed guys. It's just not working out for her.

***

And what about me? And what about you? Is there something in your life that is making you stuck and unhappy? Is this aspect of your life obvious to everyone around you, as plain as the nose on your face, like Norma's choice of the same, wrong man? If so, would you be interested in knowing what it is that everyone else sees that you don't?

Lisa drinks six cups of coffee every day but can't figure out why she has trouble sleeping at night.

Henry spends his paycheck in the bar every Friday night but complains about not having enough money for rent.

Mary complains about her weight, but never goes to the gym or cuts down on calories.

Tim opines that he never meets any girls, yet he never leaves his house.

Norma dates the same guy one decade after another.

It's so obvious what other people need to do to be happier, more content.

Assuming your friends know just as clearly what you could do to be more fulfilled, would you want them to tell you? Would you be open to their heartfelt, accurate advice?

Or are you happy dating the devil you know?

16

Run, David, Run

Just as Sauron's ring makes the wearer power mad, running marathons tends to make narcissists of us all. At the risk of using too many first person pronouns, I am going to allude in my column this week to the 15 times I have failed to qualify to run the Boston Marathon. Or as Thomas Edison said about inventing the light bulb, "I have not failed. I've just found 10,000 ways that won't work." I promise, as usual, that if you'll bear with me to the end of the page, I'll make a point about raising healthy children.

In 1980, I failed to qualify for the Boston Marathon by 19 minutes. In those days, the qualifying time was two hours and 50 minutes. Three decades later, in May of this year, I failed to qualify for the 15th time-this time I was 41 minutes off the mark.

The mark had moved, mind you. As a member of the 55 to 59 age group, I am now allowed three hours and 40 minutes to cover the 26.2 miles. But as it turns out, there's a reason the Boston Athletic Association gives you more time as you get older. Readers of my generation will know exactly what that reason is. Younger readers will find out. Five years ago when I needed to run three hours and 35 minutes, I fell short by only 97 seconds. I agree with Edison: I have not failed to qualify for the Boston Marathon. I've just found 15 ways not to.

Or as Chico Marx explained in "A Night at the Opera:" "So now I tell you how we fly to America. The first time-a we start-a, we get-a half way across when we run out of gasoline and we gotta go back. Then I take-a twice as much-a gasoline. This time we were just about to land, maybe three feet, when what do you think? We run out of gasoline again. And back we go again and get-a more gas. This time I take-a plenty gas. Wella we getta half way over ... when what do you thinka happen? We forgota the airplane."

Chico's trip is a logistical syllogism compared to my system of picking marathons, so I'll skip over nutrition, training, miles per week, the long run, speed work, the course (Note: you would think downhill would be easier; you would be wrong) and the rest of the factors that influence performance on race day and get straight to Mile 20, the "half way point," as my buddy Daniel calls it. As sparks, smoke, and little bursts of flame spew from our legs and grinding sounds emanate from our knees at the 20 mile point, Daniel whispers, "Ah. The race begins now." Hit the wall? Please. As anyone who has ever hit the wall knows, we wish it were only a wall. Typically, we hit a continent.

"A man's reach should exceed his grasp or what's a heaven for" suggested Robret Browning. But if a man reaches for the stars incessantly, he may be disappointed to learn that 22,926,149,259,000 miles-the distance to our nearest celestial neighbor-does significantly exceed the reach of his arms-no matter how consistently he does his stretching exercises.

If I qualify to run Boston, I will join a select group of athletes including:

Americans Alberto Salazar and four time winner, Bill Rodgers, my heroes when I started running in the 70s.

Kenyan Patrick Mutai, who, at 2:03:02 has completed 26.2 miles faster than anyone in the history of the Planet Earth. Ever.

Lelisa Benti, last year's winner. Who gave his medal back to the City of Boston to commemorate the victims of the bombing.

I am motivated to join this group. I train hard. I know what time I need to run. (It will come as no surprise to my old math students that I memorized the "8:11 tables" when I needed to run a 26.2 miles at 8 minutes, 11 seconds each.) In short, I know what I need to do.

I just haven't done it yet.

It's the same with your kids: they know that you would prefer that they bring home report cards filled with A grades. They know that your desires include a child who is first in her class. The following horrible joke notwithstanding, yelling at your kids is seldom effective in improving their gpa's:

Mr. Gallagher: "How did you get that piano up the stairs?"

Mr. Shean: "We tied the piano to the cat."

Mr. Gallagher: "The cat? A cat can't pull a piano up a flight of stairs!"

Mr. Shean: "We used a whip."

Parents have been asking me ever since I started teaching in the late 1970s. "How do I motivate my child?" Frequently the unspoken answer is, "She's doing the best she can with the gifts she has. If she could work harder, study more, be more organized, run faster, and get better grades then she would."

It's hurtful and harmful to judge your child in comparison to others. There is something to be said for doing the best you can, studying to the best of your ability, running as hard as you can. To allow for content children, celebrate their attitude and motivation more than their place value.

In a few months, I'll make my 16th attempt to qualify for the Boston Marathon. On that day, I'll run as fast as I can for as long as I can. Maybe I'll cough up half a lung, maybe I'll spit blood. Maybe I'll qualify for the first time and maybe I'll fail to qualify for the 16th time. Either way, at the end of 26.2, I'll be satisfied with the result, knowing that I did all I could do on that day.

I'll let you know how it goes.

17

You May Ask Yourself, Well, How Did I Get Here?

So there's this married guy on this secluded beach. And there's this attractive, young woman—not his wife—sitting behind him on a blanket rubbing coconut scented suntan oil into his back. He's talking to her about how much he loves his wife and how great their two young children are. She's talking to him about how much she loves living in the islands and what fun it is to meet traveling businessmen.

Being a gentleman, the married guy walks the attractive young woman back to her apartment. As the sun sets over the rhythmically swaying palm trees, the married guy turns to face the woman with whom he has been spending every minute that he hasn't been in meetings for the past three days of his trip. He has a decision to make: He has to decide whether or not to accept her invitation to come inside her apartment for a drink. Then he will have to decide whether or not to kiss the attractive young woman.

What should he do? Should he accept her invitation to come inside her apartment for a drink? Should the married guy kiss the attractive young woman?

As a happily married father of four, I'm rooting for no. I'm hoping for the following scenario: the married guy turns around, maybe runs into the ocean to cool off, then returns alone to his hotel room. I'm into commitment. Infidelity seldom leads anywhere good. Indiscretions—such a gentle word— harm more marriages than they help.

But first let's back up. Our married guy didn't appear "ad ovo" on the door of the attractive young woman's apartment like Athena born fully grown out of the brain of Zeus. Nor did Scotty beam down the attractive young woman from the USS Enterprise. Both the married man and the attractive young woman came from somewhere. Ignoring the singularity of the Big Bang where, to my knowledge there were no beaches and even less coconut scented suntan oil, every moment has a moment before it.

This affair started with a glance and a nod followed by a casual conversation subsequent to an invitation to lunch then a suggestion of a walk on the beach. From the blanket and the sunset, it wasn't a long way geographically or metaphorically to the doorway of the apartment.

So this issue is not what the married guy should do now, but—if you'll forgive the twisted grammar—what he should not have done before.

Contrast the married guy on the beach with my recently married friend, Mary who, on the first day of graduate school responds to a conversation from a classmate as they wait for the professor to arrive. It turns out that she and the classmate have a lot in common, shared program, shared research interests, a thousand things to talk about. Mary and her fellow graduate student feel a connection, a feeling similar to what Mary feels for her husband. So what does Mary do for the next class?

She sits across the room and doesn't respond to her pleasant classmate's subsequent attempts to engage her in conversation.

I'm not arguing that Mary is morally superior to the married guy.

I am arguing that she's smarter.

Because she doesn't have to make a difficult decision about whether or not to commit marital infidelity.

Because it is so much easier to stay out of trouble than to get out of trouble.

Envision a snarky teenager—for many of my gracious readers, little imagination will be required—who interrupts the natural flow of discourse in her home to demand breakfast in a loud, grouchy voice. What is to be done? How should the child be addressed? Should she be denied breakfast? Should she be taken aside and reprimanded? Should her mother scream back that at 15 years of age, any competent person should be capable of preparing her own breakfast and besides, they are going to be late for school? Again.

Or is this horse out of the proverbial barn? Has something gone desperately wrong along the way?

Like smoking cigarettes, the best way to stop is not to start. This child should never have been allowed to become demanding and rude.

Consider the man who, having jumped off the roof of a 30 story building, whizzes past the 20th floor exults, "So far, so good!" (In this story, the sidewalk is what is sometimes termed "the natural consequence.")

The time to dig a well is before you get thirsty. The time to decide what kind of home you want to live in is long before the kids are in their teens. The time to decide whether or not the married guy should kiss that attractive girl is long before they are alone on her doorstep.

18

Is this the Party to Whom I am Speaking?

In the generations before social media, texting and whatnot, students passed "notes." Notes were, as the name implies, pieces of paper on which messages were transcribed. In those halcyon days, "I'm going to kick your ass after school at Burger King" was about as literate a message as you were likely to receive.

One of our group, "Steve" (Steve is his real name, but for reasons that will become glaringly apparent, I don't think he reads my blog) would correct our furtive missives. Steve had an actual red pencil and a highly developed relationship with grammar. Woe to the unfortunate individual who penned, "Theirs going to be a fight, who are you rooting for?" Steve would circle "Theirs" and write "There is." Then he would write "RUN ON" in large letters as if her were solving a capital crime. If he were in a particularly expansive mood, he would explain objective case pronouns: "For whom are you going to root?" he would write in large red print. "You are going to root for 'HIM' so 'WHOM' is correct."

It will come as no surprise that Steve himself was frequently the objective pronoun in these skirmishes.

I liked Steve, perhaps not surprisingly in that I spent much of those same years trying to perfect an algorithm for multiplying three-digit numbers together in my head. It wasn't until some decades later that a dear friend had the grace to point out, "Nobody likes the math thing."

Point taken. And although I didn't get that particular memo until I was in my early thirties, it could have been worse. I might not have learned that nobody is interested in how to square numbers that end in five until much later.*

Lev Vygotsky talked about a "zone of proximal development" as the distance between what a child can do on her own and what she can do with help from adults. Stay with me here. "The zone of proximal development defines functions that have not matured yet, but are in a process of maturing, that will mature tomorrow, that are currently in an embryonic state; these functions could be called the buds of development, the flowers of development, rather than the fruits of development, that is, what is only just maturing" (Vygotsky, 1935.)

I think of the zone of proximal development as "You can't learn any Swedish from listening to people speak Swedish unless you already know some Swedish."

Just hearing Swedish isn't learning Swedish. And if you do speak some Swedish, going back to "Hi, Sven. Where is the library?" won't help either. Learning is about scaffolding, taking the next step based on a firm foundation of what you already know. A 20 word Swedish sentence in which you know 19 of the words may very well help teach you the 20th word. A 20 word Swedish sentence of which you know none of the words won't teach you anything. Except possibly to hate learning Swedish.

That Gary Larson Cartoon about what the man says to the dog and what the dog hears? That's zone of proximal development.

Because that dog isn't learning anything.

Much of what goes on in classrooms across our country is kids hating learning because they don't know what's going on. (Imagine yourself in that room with all those nice Swedish folks speaking Swedish and you don't understand a word.)

Most people can't go from algebra one class straight through to pre-calculus. Most students need to take algebra two after algebra one THEN take the more advanced class.

Your children can't run before they can walk. They can't benefit from advanced instruction before they understand the lessons leading up to it. And most importantly, if children aren't OPEN to learning, then they won't. The issue of motivation may be an advanced question, but I feel pretty strongly that nobody ever learned how to avoid "who/whom" errors from looking at Steve's scrawled letters.

First Year College Student: Excuse me, can you tell me where the library is at?

Pretentious Senior: At this university, we do not end our sentences with a preposition.

First Year College Student: Okay. Can you tell me where the library is at, asshole?

Before you try to teach your children anything, ask yourself the following question: are you modeling a love of learning or are you just showing off how much you know?

You're kids, no matter whom they are, will know there parents's reasonings.

* In the unlikely eventuality that I am mistaken and you are interested, here is the link to B. Lee Clay's wonderful website:
http://mathforum.org/k12/mathtips/beatcalc.html
Here you can learn how to square numbers in your head and much more. If, as a result of knowing "the math thing" you end up going on fewer dates, don't say I didn't warn you.

19

If a Heron Falls in a Forest

Adrienne is playing cards with his cousin, Melanie. Melanie's mom watches as the children play, occasionally, pointing to a card in her daughter's hand, giving advice, or suggesting a play. As the game progresses, Melanie's mom becomes more involved, more insistent. Ignoring the other adults at the family gathering, she makes constant recommendations and hurls invective at her daughter when the ubiquitous instructions are not followed. Melanie's mom expresses exasperation when Adrienne makes a good play; she communicates disgust when Melanie does not. In the course of a few minutes, what had been a pleasant children's game has morphed into the ninth inning of the seventh game of the World Series.

Oh, and one more thing: Melanie is 15. Her cousin, Adrienne, is 8.

Melanie, who had been having fun, is now stressed and unhappy. Her previous agenda—connecting with her cousin—is long lost. She is focused on winning or pleasing her mother or something. Enjoying a family get together is no longer on the program.

My advice for Melanie's mother is simple: Let your daughter process her own experience. Leave her alone.

What is Melanie's mother communicating by giving advice on how to beat Melanie's cousin, her junior by seven years? What will Melanie "hear" when her mother points out which card to play? Melanie will know that winning is more important than family.

Melanie will understand that she is not okay as she is.

***

Regular readers know how much I encourage healthy families to spend time in the outdoors. I can't imagine what is more powerful for families than hiking to the top of a hill and gazing out over a silent vista of trees and birds.

It doesn't take a great deal of imagination to internalize the metaphor. We like being together as a family; we like discovering what is at the top of the next trail; we can accomplish anything as long as we take it slow and stick together.

I have even allowed that not every trip is transplendent at the time, that some stories are much better when repeated years later than when experienced in real time. It's more fun to tell the story about when you were cold, wet, and lost when you're warm, dry, and found.

Here's a camping story from a dad who just about froze his two elementary school aged children: remember that night it was so cold we thought we were going to have to pack up, walk two miles back into town and find a hotel? It seemed like there was frost inside the tent and you could see your breath. But we snuggled down in our sleeping bags and got through somehow. About four in the morning the clouds cleared away and it didn't seem that cold anymore. I woke you up and you thought I was crazy. We poked our heads outside the tent and looked up to see the Milky Way overhead, a billion stars clear as water spread out behind the constellations. Nobody said anything and then we all fell asleep.

Imagine Melanie's mom on a hike in the Everglades: "look, Melanie. Look over there! See that bird? Isn't it beautiful? That bird is a blue heron! Look! The genus species for blue heron is ardeidae ardea. Blue herons were described by Linnaeus in the 18th century. And look over there! There's a turtle..."

It's great to go hiking or camping with your kids. It's even more great if you can keep quiet and let them enjoy and interpret the experience on their own. Melanie's encounter of the heron will resonate more soundly for Melanie if it isn't processed first by her mother.

What else should kids be allowed to do on their own? Within the limitations of ages and stages, probably a lot more than you think. Kids will learn from what you are and from what you do more than from what you say. Surely, by the time your children hit middle school, they should be able to do their homework on their own and advocate, if needed, for themselves. Melanie's mom, to the contrary, is in Melanie's teacher's face on a daily basis: "why did you give this assignment for homework? When did you teach this? Melanie doesn't know how to do this. Why isn't Melanie getting better grades?"

Melanie's mom is not being helpful by communicating her extreme anxiety. Melanie's mom is insuring that Melanie will never be able to do much on her own. Wouldn't it be more helpful for Melanie to develop the skill of talking to her teacher by herself? Wouldn't it be better for Melanie to learn that she will succeed or fail based on her own abilities? Wouldn't it be better for mom to just let Melanie alone?

By the time kids like Melanie come to see me, they've been poked, prodded, corrected, bothered, badgered, and annoyed to the point of madness. They haven't been allowed to look at a heron never mind process any emotions on their own. Is it any wonder than they're snippy and unresponsive? Melanie's every expression has been dissected and remarked upon. Why wouldn't she be quiet? She no longer sees the point of saying anything. For her whole life she hasn't been allowed to play a card never mind do a homework assignment or interact with a teacher for herself.

Your job as a parent is to give your child roots and wings. Your job as a parent is to allow your children to grow up strong and independent. Your job as a parent is to encourage your children to be who they are, not who you want them to be. A good way to help accomplish these goals is to allow your children to feel their feelings. If you are more invested in your 15 year-old daughter beating her eight year-old cousin at cards, if you are more concerned with your children's grades than anyone else is, it might be time to take a step back and consider whose interests are being served.

Thanks for the $20

I appreciate your patience in allowing these seemingly disparate vignettes to be woven into a workable, if not perfectly seamless, tapestry.

Part 1) The Young Realtor

Realtors who view their clients and their work as an unrelenting series of losses punctuated by rare big hits are unlikely to be satisfied or successful.

Young Realtor: Are you buying a house?

Potential Client Number One: No.

Young Realtor: Are you selling your house?

Potential Client Number Two: No.

Young Realtor: Are you buying a house?

Potential Client Number Three: Yes, but I gave the listing to my mom.

Young Realtor: Are you selling a house?

Potential Client Number Four: Yes, but I hate you and won't give you the listing.

After 95 more depressing interactions like these, the young Realtor finally closes a deal and earns two thousand dollars. If he conceptualizes his experience as 99 unpleasant time-wasting interactions followed by an hour in which he earned two thousand dollars, he is doomed to fail in his profession. Who could wake up in the morning and be cheerful about going to work knowing that the odds were 99 to 1 against earning any money? To the contrary, our Young Realtor has to say thank you to everyone who turns him down. Every time someone says "no", he has to say, "Thanks for the twenty." Every single time he asks someone to be part of a real estate transaction, he earns twenty bucks.

Part 2) As usual, Shakespeare got it right:

"If all the year were playing holidays; To sport would be as tedious as to work."
  --King Henry IV, Part 1

The following vignette may make the point: vaguely lost and soaked in dreariness, my kids and I were driving home from yet another nondescript camping trip. Once again, we had missed spotting any charismatic megafauna; indeed, we had seen no animal larger than a mosquito, a mosquito whose many relatives seemed to have joined us for the car trip home and were contentedly sucking what little blood remained from our itchy bodies. The food that wasn't undercooked on the campfire was burnt; the days that weren't unbearably hot were endlessly rainy; the card games that weren't scarred by sibling squabbles were at somebody else's picnic table because my kids couldn't seem to get through the first few minutes of any activity without bickering. We returned home covered in bug bites, mud, and tediousness. There was a trunkful of gear that needed to be cleaned, organized, and put away. What a complete bother.

If we had given up after the camping trip with the inedible food and the incessant arguments we wouldn't have gotten to subsequently have been on an interminable canoe ride at low tide through shallow brackish water in the Everglades in oppressive heat and enveloping humidity. Surrounded by muck and mangroves one boring hour after another, we saw no herons and zero wood stocks. Roseate Spoonbills? None. And don't even ask about red tailed hawks. They, along with the ospreys, had caught the last-hopefully air conditioned-train for the coast. We paddled along in silent monotony happy to know that the car was only a few hundred strokes ahead when there on the bank not fifty feet away was a gargantuan 14-foot Mouther Trucker crocodile. This primordial beast was the next door neighbor of the crocks on the National Geographic special. You know-the half ton killing machines that explode out of the Nile and take out a full grown wildebeest in a death roll. (And don't insult me by suggesting that we actually saw an alligator because only alligators inhabit Nine Mile Pond in the Everglades. I am a Florida boy, born and bred: I know the difference between an alligator and a crocodile as well as you know the difference between your mom and your dad.) This brute was huge, almost as big as the canoe. At the top of the food chain, the monster eyed us, unconcerned about puny canoeing mammals. We watched as the thousand-pound reptile finished sunning himself and lazily thundered down the bank into the lake like an F-14 landing on an aircraft carrier.

It would be only a slight exaggeration to suggest that the ground shook with each massive step. What a magnificent animal. My kids and I still talk about it, all these years later.

It's not every day you get to see a crocodile in the wild. Wow.

We can't look at all the camping trips before The Canoe Trip Where We Saw The Crocodile As Big As A School Bus as a waste of time. Nor were they practice leading up to some subsequent big event. To the contrary, each and every unexceptional trip was a twenty dollar bill tucked safely away.

***

Parents in my office frequently lament the lack of magical moments with their kids. Where is the emotional intimacy that I felt when they were little? Now that they're seniors in high school, I hardly see them. Why don't we talk anymore? Why aren't they ever at home? And when I do see them, it's all

I can do to get them to take the headphones out of their ears or to stop texting long enough for us to exchange a few sentences.

Here is some gentle advice to counteract the disconnect:

1) Set up inviolate family time. If you drive seven hours across the state to see grandma the week before Thanksgiving every year then by golly you drive seven hours across the state to see grandma at Thanksgiving this year NO MATTER WHAT is going on at the office or if you're broke or getting divorced or you were kidnapped by aliens.

Similarly, if there are no electronics at the dinner table then there are no electronics at the dinner table. Period.

2) Spend lots of time doing nothing in particular with your kids: No homework, no soccer practice, no car pool, no agenda. Just BE with your kids. (Buddhist irony intended.) Acknowledge that most of these interactions won't produce any moments worthy of the denouement of a Frank Capra film. But each evening nothing particularly noteworthy happens and your kid say, "Well, g'night, Dad" think to yourself, "Thanks for the twenty.

21

Whose Birthday is it Anyway?

In "A Nice Place to Visit" from the inaugural season of "The Twilight Zone," Sebastien Cabot welcomes Mr. Valentine, a recently deceased criminal, to a posh hotel suite. "My job is to see you get what you want, whatever it may be," says the impeccable Cabot who goes on to supply gourmet meals, attractive young women, liquor, and skeins of hundred dollar bills. Mr. Valentine, who killed a little dog and organized street gangs as a child, is surprised; he believes that he must have "done something good to make up for all the bad stuff" to have arrived in heaven. Indeed, every bet he makes at roulette wins; every coin in the slot machine hits the jackpot; every woman to whom he speaks wants to be with him.

"We'll return to Mr. Valentine in a moment," as Rod Sterling might have put it, but first let me take you through another "third door on the left", this one leading to a birthday party for a six year-old. In the shadow of multiple bounce houses, a train runs around the perimeter of the house and grounds. There are immaculately costumed characters performing skits and interacting with the hordes of feral preschoolers. Photographers and mimosas abound. The five year-old object of this white-hot spot light stands terrified at the top of a marble stairway, alternatively shrieking or mute, wishing she were somewhere else or—preferably—someone else. "Look how I sacrifice" intones her miffed parent. "I do so much for this child but she is ungrateful. Why won't she stop crying? Why is she always so sad? Does she not even know how much those clowns cost?"

What would this first grader have preferred rather than this media event masquerading as a birthday party? Toddlers want to bang on a pot with a spoon while their parents do stuff in the kitchen. Elementary school age children want to crack eggs and use the measuring cups to make brownies. How could any parent believe that this expensive, soul denying event has anything to do with the developmental needs of the child? To repeat: a birthday party for a six year-old should involve half a dozen other six year-olds and, perhaps, an art project. A twenty-foot roll of paper and some water colors should do nicely.

But back to the madness. Fast forward five years. At this birthday party a DJ—one of four at the event at the country club—instructs the pre-pubescent girls to line up on the dance floor. Shouting over the numbing bass music, the DJ then coaches the young boys to line up anonymously behind the little girls and grind their pelvises into the butts of the girls in front of them.

What are the parents thinking? Why did they set up this offensive event? Where will it all end? What is the next logical step? If you go to Dandy Bear in a limo for your seventh birthday and to Europe with a dozen of your closest friends for your fifteenth, what is left to celebrate for your 18th year? Are catered trips to Mars with a hot tub and designer drugs next on the agenda? Children appreciate relational. They want to direct their own story, not to appear as a bit player in your movie.

Let's return to the 1960 TV show: "Anything you say, Sir" says Cabot.

"But when you win every time that ain't gambling, it's charity," complains Valentine.

A pool table appears, the balls impeccable racked. Excitedly, Valentine hits the cue ball only to be disgusted when—improbably—all 15 balls drop into the pockets.

"Is something wrong?" asks Cabot.

"I can't stand it anymore," replies Valentine.

"But I don't understand, Sir."

"All right, I'll spell it out for ya, Fats. I'm bored, bored. There's no excitement over here, no kicks."

""I thought you liked gambling."

"It don't mean anything if it's all set up in advance… And the dames. I never thought I'd get bored with beautiful dames."

Valentine has an idea. He determines that he'd prefer to be in "the other place."

"Just between you and me, Fats, I don't think I belong here. I don't think I fit it."

"Oh, nonsense, of course you do."

"Look, I don't belong in heaven, see? I wanna go to the other place."

"Heaven," replies Cabot. "Whatever gave you the idea that you were in heaven, Mr. Valentine? This IS the other place."

And the trombone music swells as Valentine, unable to open the door, realizes where he is. Cabot's maniacal laughter gives way to the Twilight theme music.

I'll let Rod Sterling's narration spell it out for you, "Now he's got everything he ever wanted. And he's going to have to live with it for all eternity. In the twilight zone."

Your children aren't criminals. Don't punish them by giving them that which they don't want. Let them make their own meaning in a world whose boundaries they can understand and appreciate. An adolescent who works an after school job to buy a bicycle will appreciate the ten-speed more than a kid who is given an expensive new car. Allow your children to earn the things they want. Reward them by fulfilling their needs, but not giving in to their wants. In the meantime, don't even pretend that these over-the-top parties have anything to do with what is in the long term best interests of the birthday girl.

22

I'll Let You Be in My Dream if I Can Be in Yours

Not one to name drop but I have to tell you that a buddy of mine is one of the preeminent screen writers in the country. He has sold scripts to Stephen Spielberg; he has written movies that you have seen. "Bryan" is top of the food chain in Hollywood, which is why I believe him when he says that no movie about an underdog sports team that doesn't win can be produced. (Hey, I'm not going to use the "L" word in a family publication). Go ahead and add your favorites to this list: "Bad News Bears," "Dodge Ball," "Space Jam," "Mighty Ducks," "Sandlot," that unwatchable Sylvester Stallone film about soccer. The list is as long as the movies are tedious. To enjoy M*A*S*H, a better film, you have to overlook that the "good" doctors use syringes to incapacitate the other players. In Hollywood films, take it to the bank, the "good" guys always win.

When my buddy, in high level talks with studio executives, dared to suggest that it might be more interesting, never mind more accurate, to allow a film to end without the triumphant congratulatory champagne immersion, he was told categorically that it would never happen. "That movie won't be made," he was told. "No one will pay money to see it."

To see people who don't always win, you may wish to take a walk around an actual neighborhood—the one in which you live should do nicely.

Because the tricky bit is that unlike darkened theaters, in real life classrooms, in real life job interviews, and in real life sporting events, not quite everyone emerges victorious. The cameras may follow the gold medalists but let's do the arithmetic: as you root fervently for golden haired, flexible Flossie Flip-flop to nail her dismount, aren't you cheering just as vehemently for Stacey Somersault to land on her butt? Because there will be three spaces on the podium in Rio, just like there were in London.

Another easy arithmetic question: What do 63 of the 64 teams in the "March Madness" tournament have in common? Put your pencils down. That's right. Sixty-three teams go home without the big trophy. This just in: not everybody wins.

A reader whom I respect responded to one of my "Give it all you've got. Then go home content" columns with the following comment:

"Thinking 'I did my best' is poor consolation for continuing in a deadening job instead of passing an important exam."

The problem is that not everyone can pass the exam any more than everyone can fit on the podium at the Olympics. SOMEONE has to have that lousy job. SOMEONE has to not win. SOMEONE has to go home.

That the camera never follows these folks doesn't mean that they no longer exist.

For a historical context, consider Germany who "came in second" in the First World War. It is my understanding that, not having won that particular event, they were not satisfied with the outcome of the contest and, subsequently, allowed their discontent to cause the death of, among others, 30 million Russians.

Rooting for your child to get "Student of the Month" in her kindergarten class is natural. Understanding that those 19 other children are somebody else's kids is necessary. Unless you can make more months, I want to know what happens to the kids who don't win. Do you think they internalize, "Gee, I better work harder, be more social, do more homework, and behave better so that I can win next month?" Neither do I. To the contrary, I think those other kids envision a Scarlett 'L' emblazoned on their chest.

Many gentle readers will recognize the title of this entry from "Talkin' World War III Blues" from "The Freewheelin' Bob Dylan" from 1963.

Here's what Bruce Springsteen sang in "Atlantic City" in 1982:

Down here it's just winner and losers
And don't get caught on the wrong side of that line.
Well, I'm tired of comin' out on the losin' end
So, Honey, last night I met this guy and I'm gonna do a little favor for him.

The paradigm has to change. In the classroom, in politics, and on the street, we have to realize that allocating all our resources exclusively to the most able…

… is a losing proposition.

23

Nice Day

Not so many years ago on vacation in Aspen, my parents changed hotel rooms. I forget why although I do remember that this was in the days before cell phones. Connected inadvertently to the room where my folks no longer were, I spoke at length to a Mrs. Stone about her grandchildren, Alabama football, the weather in the mountains, and other gentle concerns of the day. Sensing that we might not agree about politics or religion, we both graciously skirted those potentially disagreeable topics in favor of more congenial connections. We talked about the Rocky Mountain Trail near her hotel, we chatted about the big western sky, we schmoozed about animals wild and domesticated. If I remember correctly, she may have shared with me a recipe for corn muffins. Twenty minutes in to our communication, it occurred to me that I still hadn't spoken to my parents and that I might be intruding on her vacation. I said, "Mrs. Stone, I can't begin to tell you how much I'm enjoying our conversation, but you have to admit that this is basically just a wrong number."

"Honey," she answered with impeccable Southern cadence. "We're the Stones from Tuscaloosa." She paused as if that explained everything then continued: "We can talk to a stump."

***

In my part of Miami, I frequently feel like I would have a better time of it if I did indeed try to communicate with dead trees rather than attempt to engage my neighbors in conversation. When I reach out to a fellow citizen, as I frequently do, it seems they are as likely to scramble inside, bar the door, and reach for a shotgun as they are to participate in a short chat. My agenda is a brief dialogue: "How 'bout them Dolphins?" "Isn't this the hottest summer you can remember?" "How's the family?" But I get the feeling that my neighbors are waiting for the hit: "Let me try to convert you to my cultish religion." "I want to put my hand on your behind." "Would you like to buy an overpriced and worthless product or service, a Ronco 'Bass-o-Matic,' perhaps?

Having no agenda other than, "It's a nice day for a chat," I am frequently surprised by the running and hiding behaviors of my neighbors, but I don't fault them. In the big city there are any number of telemarketers and other unwelcome intrusions into family time. I could be anybody; how can they tell that I'm a chatty middle aged man walking a dog rather than the next psycho headline?

With folks with whom you already have a relationship, a great gift can be the "no agenda" phone call. If every time you called a friend, you tried to sell him something it wouldn't be long before you got the answering machine rather than a hello when you called. Everybody prefers the "just thinking of you" to the "three easy payments of $26.95" call.

It's the same with the kids. If your children are expecting to hear, "Do your homework" and "Clean your room" because all you ever say to them is "Do your homework" and "Clean your room," it won't be long before you're getting blank stares no matter what you say.

Schedule some "no agenda" time with your kids. And don't tell me that you asked your child to have a catch and you got turned you down in favor of "Blood, Blood, Blood, Shoot, Shoot, Shoot, Kill, Kill, Kill." "The past is close behind" as Dylan sang in "Tangled Up in Blue." If the last time you threw a ball with your kid, you managed to communicate "Keep your eye on the ball, damn it, if you don't make it to the major leagues we're all going to starve and die!" your kid picked up on that message, take it to the bank.

Even a stray dog knows if it's been tripped over or kicked.

A better message—which can certainly go unspoken—is that we enjoy being together. The sun is shining; we have our health; and the ball make such a nice "thwump" sound when it hits the glove.

Yes, the future is uncertain; sure, you might not make the varsity team never mind the major league; and, there is no doubt but that tomorrow we might all get run over by a bus. But for right now, we're just parent and child, no conversation, no agenda, no hurry. Just tossing a ball back and forth. What could be better than that?

I don't know—remember we only spoke for 20 minutes—but I like to believe that Mrs. Stone from Tuscaloosa would agree.

24

Can Do

Teachers across the country are being bombarded with the following narrative from well-meaning but horribly misguided parents: "Don't tell my daughter that she got a 'B' on the test. We don't want to damage her self-esteem. We will help her more with her homework, we promise. It's just that she's so delicate and she doesn't have a good sense of herself because she has an August birthday and her older sister is so much smarter. If our younger daughter finds out that she got a 'B' she'll give up studying and I know you don't want her to quit on herself. Please tell her she got an 'A on the test'."

These parents and this conversation have spread like algae blooms across grade level and into public and private schools. I'm not arguing that your children's institutions are perfect, that their teachers are flawless, or that students shouldn't get the support that they need. I have written extensively on how parents are the first and most important teachers for their children. I acknowledge that teachers can be insensitive, demanding, unfair, or even rude. But contrast the lawn mower parents above with the following statement culled from an adolescent's recent experience:

"Yeah, the water was rising pretty fast and it didn't seem like there was a viable way for the rest of the folks to get down off the rock under the overhang without slipping. You know how Uncle Nate's knees are and it was so dark we couldn't see the moss on the rocks. He wouldn't have been able to see much with the rain blowing so hard and I didn't want him to end up slipping and dropping eight feet into the river. So I made three trips to get everybody's back pack and then I went back again to help Nate and the rest of the people down."

"Weren't you exhausted, hungry, and terrified after hiking all day and being lost all that way from the campsite?"

"Yeah, I guess. If I'd thought about it, maybe. But somebody had to get my family out of there and I didn't think I could count on air support."

If self-esteem results from overcoming—not avoiding—failure, where do you think heroism comes from?

How is your child going to have the intestinal fortitude to help his Uncle Nate off a ledge if you've argued every grade for him all the way through school? The alternative—allowing your son to get a B or allowing him to advocate for himself about why he should have a different grade—is vastly preferable. And if I may ask a frank question: WHY IS IT SO IMPORTANT TO YOU THAT YOUR CHILD GET ALL A GRADES?

Because your child's life IS going to involve some tricky bits. If he's not stuck on a rock above a river in the dark, he'll be faced with some intractable problem somewhere along the way. Don't you want your kids to have the skills to overcome adversity? Where do you think these skills are going to come from?

Your child may be picked last for softball, fail her driver's test, or be rejected by a favored suitor. You can't protect her but you can prepare her. You can't give her the answer but you can give her the skill. The best preparation to deal with big disappointments as an adult is to practice overcoming smaller disappointments as a child.

Psychically, one of the worst things you can do as a parent is to feel your child's feelings for her, soften every blow, rescue her from every uncomfortable situation, enable her to build a castle on shifting sand. Support, listen, and help her problem solve, yes. Deny her the chance to overcome problems in her own way, no. And whatever you do, under no circumstances should you be talking to your child's fourth grade teacher about a 'B' on a test.

Chances are, your children aren't all that fragile. Unless you make them that way. Unless you want them to be.

25

496 Years and Counting

Imagine a Protestant locked in a dim, dank room with a Catholic. The chairs are hard and uncomfortable, the lighting poor. Outside where the sun is shining, children are frolicking in the surf as their contented parents sip drinks with little umbrellas in them. The protestant and the catholic can come out of the moldy room when one convinces the other, converts him to the contrasting point of view. Until the transition takes place, the protestant and the catholic can talk as long as they like, but can only send out for food from a restaurant whose menu options include grease fried in fat and a puree of toad parts special.

Can you imagine this conversation lasting 500 years? I can envision just such a schedule. Because indeed the conversation has lasted just shy of 500 summers. Catalyzing the Protestant Reformation, Luther tacked those 95 theses on the door in 1517, coming up on half a millennia ago. A quick glance at the headlines around the globe would suggest that the chat is not going to end any time soon: the Catholics are not going to become Protestants; the Protestants are not going to convert to Catholicism.

***

A buddy of mine in his 50s was complaining about his second wife. They're going through a rough patch and it's pretty clear the marriage is heading toward dissolution. "If only she would listen to me." he says. "If only she would do what I say."

This just in: she's not.

"But, it's so obvious," he goes on. "We don't have money for this. We barely have enough money for that."

My gentle readers will forgive me if I had faded out by this point in the conversation and—thinking about watching my children play on the beach—wasn't listening closely enough to remember the ponderous details.

"Why can't she just see things my way, do what I want?" he went on. "I've been divorced before, I don't want to get divorced again, but she just won't listen to reason."

Were I a different sort of fellow, I might have pointed out that the only person at the scene of both accidents was the person speaking.

***

As parents, what makes us think that we can control the choices of our children by yelling at them? Don't misunderstand: I agree that you're right about your children. I'm not questioning the accuracy of your beliefs. You're older and you know better. I'm just wondering if yelling at them is the way to effect positive change.

Is there another way to influence our kids to become successful and content as adults? First and foremost, we have to focus exclusively on what is in their best interest. Not everyone can play in the NBA. If I, a paunchy, balding, middle aged man can finally come to terms with the desperately unpleasant reality that LeBron James need not worry about my usurping his position, then surely you can accept that not everyone can matriculate at Princeton. Not everyone has the academic chops to be admitted—which is just as well.

Only a subset of the three million high school grads in 2014 can fit on a campus with 1400 first-year students.

Haranguing your kids that the alternative to heading to New Jersey is plummeting down the road to perdition and sloth is contraindicated.

You have less control, influence, and authority than you think you do. The serenity prayer isn't just for those of us who mourn the poor choices of loved ones.

The president of the United States, a man who is, by all accounts, more powerful and smarter than you or I, mentioned recently that he cannot control the congress. You have less authority than he does. You think my kids are easier to control than are those 435 congress people? You haven't met my kids.

Here's what you can do: be who you are. Let your kids be who they are.

In the meantime, you can model. If you would prefer that your children read books rather than play video games, get off your computer and scarf down a paperback. If you would prefer that your children resolve conflict with calm reasoning rather than volcanic outbursts, consider screaming less loudly the next time a family decision doesn't go your way. If you want your kids to be healthy, consider putting down that double bacon cheeseburger and the martini. Here. Have a nice carrot. And don't even tell me that you only smoke pot when your children are out of the house and that your children don't know that you take the occasional puff. If you smoke pot, then your children already know that you do.

They told me. They've told everybody. Take it to the bank.

Physics 101: "186,282 miles per second; it's not just a good idea. It's the law."

Bad Parenting 101: "Do as I say, not as I do."

If you feel like every day is a battle with your kids, an unending diatribe of unrealized expectations and disappointments that could go on for 496 years, maybe it's time to walk out of the small dark room into the sunshine and the children playing on the beach.

26

Strategy

Which small colleges in the Pacific Northwest have a competitive women's varsity volleyball team and a strong musical theater department? Which Midwestern universities have support for students with learning differences and good Greek life? Which colleges have the best four-year and six-year graduation rates? Which colleges have the highest percentage of alumni contributions? Which liberal arts colleges will take a chance on a hard-working B-/C+ student who is passionate about creative writing?

My wonderful professional organization—the Independent Educational Consultants Association—supports a list serve where these and other obscure questions are answered promptly and graciously. Members support one another and are eager to lend a helping email. Indeed, IECA members claim that there are no "data driven" questions that we can't answer quickly and accurately.

But there is a subset of admissions questions that concerns me. Matching students and institution is a good thing. Conferring unfair advantage is not. Whenever I hear the word "strategy" or the phrase "what do admissions officers prefer?" I cringe because I know what's coming. The giveaway is "I don't want to game the system, but…" Invariably the next sentence includes the word "disclosure" as in: "My son has severe learning differences, gets accommodations in high school, and takes tests untimed, but we don't want to tell the college because his chances of being admitted will be less." "My son got arrested for committing a burglary after smoking pot but his attorney says that the record can be expunged. Does the student have to disclose?" And the most common: "My daughter doesn't have the profile to be admitted to First Choice U; how do we get her in anyway?"

Is the child who committed the burglary sorry he did something wrong? Or is he just sorry that he got caught? Does the boy with learning differences want to be admitted to college? Or are we interested in his success once he matriculates? Does the girl with the credentials a bit below the mean for F.C.U. (Go, First Choice University!) understand that it's not the dog in the fight, but the fight in the dog?

Loving parents know, "Help your daughter acquire the SKILLS so that she will be successful wherever she ends up matriculating." If she is admitted to Amherst, she needs to be able to function at Amherst; if she ends up at Colby (Go, Mules!) she needs to have the background to succeed at Colby.

There is something worse than Tommy being rejected from the University of Chicago. Coming home from U. C. after half a semester because Tommy doesn't have the skills to be successful in the classroom? That's worse.

Remember that kid in high school who spent hours inventing and implementing ways to cheat on every exam? He would design and disguise elaborate formula sheets. He would hide papers up his sleeves and in his shoes. In the days before instantaneous electronic communication, he even used the time difference between New York and San Francisco to get a jump on questions on a standardized test administered nationwide.

"If he spent as much time studying as he does cheating," his teachers and parents lamented, "he would get perfect scores on every test." If he would just put that creative intellect to work studying instead of scamming.

The analogy to admissions is clear: Smart kids who know how to turn off the electronics so they can study are the ones who do well. No matter where they go to college. Kids who game the system so that they can be admitted to a college where they don't have the skills? Not so much.

It's the reality rather than the indicia of ability that matters.

Rather than finding a teacher who will "sign off" on service hours that don't actually exist, why not do the work? Rather than asking "How many hours of community service should I do to look good for this college?" consider instead "What are the values for my family?" Rather than signing up to be a "paper member" of clubs in which you have no actual interest, why not commit your time to the activities that are truly important to you?

Remember that lovely girl in high school who had that wicked crush on that hunky guy? Remember how she pretended to like drinking beer and watching football so that he would be attracted to her?

Remember how unhappy she was after they were married when it turned out that, in reality, she enjoys neither beer nor football? Remember their difficult divorce? Remember how confused and unhappy their children were?

I'll ask Polonius to bring us home from Act I, scene iii of "Hamlet." His son, Laertes, is about to head out, not to college necessarily, but he is going down to the dock to jump on a ship. In the four hundred something years since Polonius gave this advice to his son there are still no truer words.

… to thine ownself be true,
And it must follow, as the night the day,
Thou canst not then be false to any man.

How many of us as parents are giving our children the advice to be both truthful and able? Helping our kids to have both skill and truthfulness beats the heck out of helping them lie and cheat so they end up in the wrong place.

27

If at First You Don't Succeed

What no one acknowledges—parents, teachers, administrators, elected officials—is what every high school student already knows. The great unspoken, tacit agreement throughout our culture in general and our schools in particular, is that every student can learn every subject at the same level of proficiency. The reality is that in our great land of opportunity, all students may be created equal, but in trigonometry class, differences may easily be observed.

Consider a developmentally delayed youngster for whom even relatively simple acts—tying a shoe lace, understanding these blog posts—are a trial. Surely this youngster should not be expected to learn the binomial theorem. Without knowing the second term of $(2x + 3y)^5$, she can live a contented life as a chimney sweep or TV news anchor. But only if her expectations are in keeping with her preferences and abilities. If she is forced to sit in a room until she understands where $240 x^4 y$ came from, we may have to send out for some large number of pizzas.

Which is not to give anyone an excuse to slack. Those who can, should. But after a point, "try, try again" must evolve into "but don't be a damn fool about it." Even "never give up" is a poor motto for many professions, skydiving among them.

Consider the author of the best-selling humanities text book in the country. The author, by her own admission, could not tell you the quadratic formula from a Formula One race car. Admittedly, writing the best-selling humanities textbook in the country is akin to crowning "One Life to Live" as the best of the day time soap operas. (At the risk of explaining the joke, I wouldn't recommend committing to any day time soap opera, best or otherwise, nor would I want to try to feed a family on the paltry earnings from a text book—even a brilliant, best-selling one.) The point—"finally" you might say—is that had my mom been forbidden from pursuing higher education because of her inability to do much math, our world would be a poorer place. It should also be noted that there has not been one reference to the binomial theorem in ten editions of The Art of Being Human.

The question is not "should everyone be given the opportunity to learn the binomial theorem." Like, Duh. Come sit over here; I'll teach you the binomial theorem right now. Of course, everyone should have the opportunity to learn the binomial theorem. The question is whether or not those of you who, like my mom, can't learn the binomial theorem should be squashed, prohibited from getting a graduate degree in some other discipline just because you can't.

One of my favorite students failed geometry for the third time recently. He said he just couldn't learn it, that he forgot the theorems as soon as he thought he had memorized them, that there was no way he could possibly get through the course. His parents, counselors, teachers, and I listened patiently and thoughtfully, and then, with one voice, responded with these two words: "BULL" and "SHIT! We went on to say, "THERE IS NO REASON IN HEAVEN OR ON EARTH WHY YOU CAN'T PASS THIS GEOMETRY COURSE, YOU WRETCHED SLOTH! TAKE GEOMETRY FOR THE FORTH TIME, DIM BULB, AND DON'T GIVE ME ANY LAME ASS EXCUSES, NOW DROP AND GIVE ME TWENTY!"

Gentle guidance—equal parts sensitive and mild—is what all good educators are known for. Needless to say, the fourth time was the charm and the kid was pretty well pleased to have gotten the job done.

But were this child to come back to me next year and ask for advice about whether or not he should sign up for a course in differential equations, I would mindfully suggest that he was cuckoo for cocoa puffs and then check his forehead for fever and cerebral subdural hematomas whatever those are because enough is enough already and not every student can learn every subject at every level.

The biggest lie in education is disguised in plain sight in statistics like this one. (Read with haughty English accent.) "At glorious Fish Wallow University, 97 percent of our pre-medical students are admitted to graduate schools of medicine." Gloriosky! Then all I have to do is enroll at F. W. U. and I get to go straight to med school? Not so fast, me Bucko! Because what the statisticians have deftly left out is the large number of students at glorious F. W. U. who aren't included in the stat. And a large number of kids are indeed excluded from the alleged 97% med school acceptance rate because organic chemistry at Fish Wallow produces more history majors than it does doctors. In order to be defined as a pre-medical student as Fish Wallow, you have to get through organic chemistry. Which not everyone does.

The biggest question in education is when to admit that further instruction will have no positive effect.

It's lovely to think of Edward Jame's Olmos portraying Jaime Escalante in that fine 1988 film, "Stand and Deliver" in which all the low income kids work hard all semester and then pass the advanced placement calculus exam. It's another thing to think that this sort of result happens frequently with any group of students at any school.

As happy as I was for my student who passed Geometry on the fourth try, I would not have forbid him to pursue other academic passions had he failed.

28

Everyone has to Believe in Something; I believe I'll Have Another Lemonade

Two generations ago it was a big deal to come back to your dorm room and find a tie hanging over the doorknob. The implications were as staggering as they were rare: a tie on the door meant your roommate was with a girl in your dorm room! An actual, flesh and blood, honest to goodness girl! "Get lost," the tie explained. "There's a girl in here!"

It might have seemed possible that somewhere in the next 50 years under some set of alien circumstances that somehow, some way there might be men at the summit of Everest. Maybe someday a man would run a mile in under four minutes. Who knows? Anything is possible. Heck, conceivably men might someday walk on the moon. But your roommate with a girl in his room? Now <u>that</u> was unlikely.

Yet a scant 50 years later, hookups in college dorm rooms are the common rule rather than the obscure exception. The Sunday morning "walk of shame" across campus is no longer worthy of remark.

The purpose of my gentle diatribe this week is not to decry young adults being sexually active. Indeed, who could argue for the other end of the spectrum? Who would suggest that woman getting married in 1919, say, should not know where babies came from?

My argument is more subtle than "young people didn't know enough about reproductive biology a century ago" or "young people know too much about casual sex today." Nor am I arguing for moderation or condoms, although I certainly favor both. Instead I am lobbying for an assortment of choices. Just as the young couple who are lucky enough to have found each other should be allowed to have their moment alone, so too should the returning boarder be allowed unimpeded access to his digs. As unlikely as it sounds, he might want to study. Or sleep uninterrupted. Three people in a dorm room is not only a crowd but crowded. It's not the odd man who should be out; it's the amorous couple who should seek accommodation elsewhere.

You'll have to consider other venues, gentle readers, to discover that our college-aged children are having more sex than ever before but enjoying it less. My point is only that developmentalists (a fancy word for my graduate degree: my M.S. in Developmental Psychology could be characterized as "home economics with numbers") talk about "ages and stages". Not all children are potty trained twenty minutes after their third birthday; not all children learn to read by the start of first grade. It is said that Einstein didn't speak fluently until age nine. Surely some young adults are ready for satisfying physically intimate relationships during the college years. And others not. We should allow our children to make their choices unimpeded.

Whether or not college campuses are joining the dictionary as the only place where "intercourse" comes before "introduction", I turn our attention now to campus drinking. Having journeyed to some 200 colleges and having taken the official tour at most of these, I am intimately well acquainted with the company line. The articulate, walking-backwards, tour guide recites, "Sure, there are a few kids on campus who drink alcohol. But there is no pressure to do so."

Maybe. But combine "misery loves company" with "the more the merrier" and the likelihood of lonely sober kids increases. You could get through the

104

weekend without drinking; you would need to have a good sense of yourself beforehand though. Consider this conversation between an unfortunately overweight young man and a young woman who had recently matriculated at his college.

Young Man: You're sure you don't want a glass of wine?

Young woman: No, thank you.

Young Man: You don't drink?

Young Woman: No.

Young Man: Why don't you drink?

Young Woman: Why don't you exercise?

For every strong, self-assured, young woman who knows who she is and what she wants, there is another first year college student who will be influenced by the "everyone else is doing is" zeitgeist.

We allow our college-age kids to pick their majors; we allow our college-age kids to pick their roommates. As parents and educators we should let our college-age kids know that we allow them to choose sobriety and discretion as well.

29

I Don't Want to Die Stupid

Note the importance of the punctuation mark or lack thereof. A grouchy hiker arguing over the choice of paths might exclaim, "I don't want to die, Stupid." There is no comma in my sentence: "I don't want to die stupid." I'm using "stupid" as an adjective, not as a proper noun.

I'm not sure exactly what questions are going to be on the final exam, but I'm pretty sure, "How many consecutive reruns of 'Sex and the City' did you watch?" and "Do you know who Jennifer Aniston is dating?" will not be among them.

On the other hand, I think there may be questions of the form, "Did you read ___?" To which a response of "no" might prompt an incredulous deity to respond, "In an entire lifetime, you never got around to reading ___? Really?

Not wishing to cause consternation among the celestial, I have to give some thought as to what will fit in that blank?

Here's some sobering, if inescapable algebra: If I read x books a year and I live for y more years, then I get to read x times y more books. It might be time to choose the titles with a little more care. Which is not to say I regret or resent the hours I spent with my mistresses—John Irving, Carl Hiaasen, James Elroy—but it might be time to devote to my beloved wife. It is time to return to reading classics.

After whoring around, stealing, and drinking with Falstaff for years, Prince Hal ascends to the throne as King Henry IV. When Falstaff greets him, the King replies, "I know thee not, Old Man." Similarly, it might be time for me to put on my big boy pants and read real books again. Maybe I should start with Shakespeare's King Henry IV.

A buddy of mine refers to me as a—how did he put it? Oh, yes, I remember now—"pretentious twit." "You're amassing a list of titles the way a miser collects gold coins. You can't take it with you, you know."

"Oh, yeah?" I replied.

"And the list of subjects about which you know nothing dwarfs the few little islands of competence, you've managed to cobble together."

"Nuh uh." I said.

"You haven't read Tolstoy or Dostoevsky. Your knowledge of non-Western literature fits in a thimble with room left over. You don't know Plato from Pluto"

"Do too," I said.

"You don't even speak any languages in addition to your limited proficiency with English." He continued.

"I was trying to limit the discussion to books" I answered.

Ignoring for the moment whether I should acquire some kinder friends, I would argue that there is something to be said for reading classics so as not to die stupid. Here's how Harper Lee addressed a similar issue in 1962. The only backstory you may have forgotten is that 12 year-old, Jem, is reading to Mrs. Dubose, a mean spirited, elderly, terminally-ill neighbor. Scout, the naïve narrator, describes the first time the children are in the scary, bleak room with Mrs. Dubose:

There was a marble-topped washstand by her bed; on it were a glass with a teaspoon in it, a red ear syringe, a box of absorbent cotton, and a steel alarm clock standing on it.

Subsequently, the children's father comes by to pick them up after they have finished reading.

"Do you know what time it is, Atticus?" [Mrs. Dubose] said. "Exactly fourteen minutes past five. The alarm clock's set for five-thirty. I want you to know that."

It suddenly came to me that each day we had been staying a little longer at Mrs. Dubose's, that the alarm clock went off a few minutes later every day, and that she was well into one of her fits by the time it sounded. Today she had antagonized Jem for nearly two hours with no intention of having a fit.

...

"I have a feeling that Jem's reading days are numbered," said Atticus.

"Only a week longer, I think," she said, "just to make sure..."
...

When she dies, the children finally learn why they were forced to spend so many tedious afternoons with her:

"Mrs. Dubose was a morphine addict," said Atticus. "She took it as a pain-killer for years. The doctor put her on it. She'd have spent the rest of her life on it and died without so much agony, but she was too contrary—"

...

Perhaps mountain climbers and ultra-marathoners can appreciate Mrs. Dubose's accomplishment.

If Mrs. Dubose can kick opium, surely I can beat ignorance.

What is the legacy that you want to leave for your children? What do you want them to have to remember you by when you've gone on to that great library in the sky? Do you think they will look back on their dearly departed parents and remark: "Remember that time at the mall we were in the checkout line at the clothing store and we read that article about that famous woman who cheated on her boyfriend and went out with that sports star and then he dumped her?"

Wouldn't you agree that it is more likely that your kids will wish they could say, "My dad modeled for us his love of reading and his love of learning"?

And, speaking of addiction, for goodness gracious sakes, whatever you do, you and your kids need to put down those electronics. If crotchety, old Mrs. Dubose can kick morphine and if I can get back to reading literature, surely you and your family can go one day each week without your glowing rectangles and pulsating screens.

You and your children can live for a few hours without texting and email. Set a steel alarm clock on the marble-topped washstand if you have to.

30

R-O-N-G

"I'm not usually one to complain, but when a hotel advertises hot and cold running champagne, you don't expect the Jacuzzi to run out of Dom Perignon so quickly. Not to mention that I specifically asked for imported cucumbers to be placed on my eyes at the spa so you can imagine my disappointment when I discovered domestic fruit being used. When things start to go wrong, it's just one thing after another. And don't even get me started on the service on the airlines. If those snarky flight attendants with their attitude is what passes for first class, I don't even want to imagine what goes on in business.

"I am also having trouble with my husband. I suppose he's trying his best, but what a lout. I TOLD him that I wanted a vacation to get away from it all. Did I say I wanted a vacation to get away from SOME of it? No, I did not. So you can imagine my outrage when we ended up on this non-descript island in the South Seas that nobody has ever heard of. Then he gets a room on the top floor so we have to wait for ages to get the elevator to take us out to the beach. Then he changes us to a suite on the ground floor but now we don't have a view of the horizon. And the hotel staff? Don't even ask. Some of them spoke five or six languages but not English. If you're going to learn a foreign language, why wouldn't you learn English, the language that I speak? I may not know any other languages, but at least I know English.

"Speaking of inept employees, those buffoons at the hotel remind me of the teachers in my son's school. The teachers there are supposed to TEACH my child. We pay good money. Sure my son misses classes. But he's up late playing video games and he says some of those classes are boring anyway and that the teachers don't allow him to learn the way he wants. The teachers are paid to teach him not to be the sleeping police telling him that he has to stay awake in class. They should teach my child when he wants to learn. When he's awake obviously. What's the point of trying to teach him when he's sleeping or stoned? (Maybe he shouldn't be sneaking off campus to buy pot, but if the school didn't really want him to smoke pot they would put guard dogs by the eight foot fence at the perimeter of the campus. Duh!)

"When we were choosing schools, they told us that this school was supportive of children with different learning styles. Supportive? Hah! It's nothing of the kind. My son isn't learning anything. And worse than the fact that he's not learning anything at all, they give him bad grades. Can you believe it? Those feckless teachers aren't teaching him then, to add insult to injury, they give him bad grades. As if it's my son's fault that he doesn't do homework. How many times do I have to tell them that he's up late playing video games?"

***

How many of us as loving parents make a similar mistake to the one made by the (admittedly unbearable) narrator above? Hopefully, none of us is so spoiled rotten as to be demeaning to hard working hotel employees. But what are we communicating to our kids when we openly deride their teachers? Admittedly some teachers are more sensitive than others, some are more open to kids with different learning styles, and some teachers are doubtless downright inept.

But what is the point of going on and on about how horrible the classroom is? If the teachers are imperfect, shouldn't we take responsibility for educating our own children? To allow our kids to play video games to the exclusion of reading books is to set ourselves up for meaningless complaint.

Like the boy who killed both his parents then threw himself on the mercy of the court because he was an orphan, allowing our kids to avoid learning because the teachers are imperfect is a bad strategy.

Kids should be expected to make it work, to pull themselves up by their bootstraps, to "make it do or do without" as a slogan of a previous generation suggested. And if the student fails to get through a class, let him learn from the experience. "Success doesn't come from *avoiding* failure, but from *overcoming* failure."

And parenting from a hotel room never works, no matter where the cucumbers come from.

31

Silent Safety

Disgruntled ex-lovers can now post inappropriate pictures of a previous inamorata on a number of websites designed specifically for this unpleasant purpose. In a world where a photo of your daughter in the nude or worse could be seen by anyone with a computer, it comes as no surprise that parents feel out of control. We want to protect our children. What could be more natural?

The tricky bit is that those who want to harm our children are no longer at a distance of a day's ride into town. Stranger danger is now only a few clicks away. Like in a horror movie, the bad guys are in the house.

So, under these dire circumstances, proper etiquette may be the least of our issues on a given day and no, using a salad fork won't keep your children safe. Process addictions—cigarettes, oxycontin, vodka, lottery tickets, excessive video gaming, marijuana—are all readily available whether or not you accept the following gentle guidance about proper conversation. At the risk of writing an "Advice-Lite" chapter, here are some suggestions:

When talking about how great your children are, don't.

I know, I know. This instruction sounds not only mild, but stupid. How did we get from the possibility of inappropriate photos of loved ones to an admonition not to brag about our kids? I promise I'll connect the dots. But first tell me how you feel about comments like these:

1) I just can't seem to gain a pound. No matter what I eat, the weight just comes right off. I have a milkshake almost every night. It doesn't matter. Celery and low calorie food? No thank you! Fried chicken with cheese cake for me. I never gain weight!

2) Of course, I've heard about how many women have trouble with child birth—36 hours of labor, Caesarian sections, pain, prescribed narcotics, and whatnot—but for me it was just two pushes and done. I hardly felt a thing and then I held my perfect son in my arms. I just don't see what all the fuss is about. The OB said I should stay in the hospital overnight, but I was ready to go home an hour after giving birth.

3) I just don't understand these people who have unsupportable debt or are underwater with their mortgages. They must buy 60-inch televisions and eat restaurant sushi for every meal. We bought our home years ago. Now, it's worth ten times what we paid for it. We got a 15-year mortgage and paid it off early with some money my mother-in-law left us.

And now the most relevant to good parenting, not just polite conversation:

4) My Jonny won the spelling bee again this year for the third time. He is so smart. He hardly studies and he always gets the best grades in his class.

Consider the audience. If you're bragging about your neuro-typical son to the mother of an autism spectrum child, might she feel just the least bit disconcerted? Surely your friend wants what is best for you and clearly she shares your joy in your son's victories and honors. She just might not want to hear about it quite so often.

Because did it ever occur to you that you might just be lucky? Sure, you read Goodnight Moon to your little one. Yes, you withstood the urge to scream at your toddler when he painted the couch. Yes, you've worked hard to put food on the table.

But just the same, would you consider shutting up about it?

Maybe you could just smirk quietly.

And if being a better friend isn't reason enough to stop bragging about your daughter's victories in the soccer playoffs, how about the benefits to your child? If you keep your mouth mostly shut...

1) Your kids will know they are loved for who they are not for what they do.

2) They will be less likely to cheat to meet your expectations

3) Your kids will know they are loved for who they are not for what they do.

4) They will feel better about themselves.

5) Your children will internalize your high expectations.

6) Your kids will know they are loved for who they are not for what they do.

As a result, your kids will be less susceptible to process addictions trying to ensnare them. Drugs and alcohol are less attractive to kids who are loved and valued for who they are.

Who would have thought that a big step in keeping our children safe is keeping our mouths shut?

32

Madness

Between "Kind Hearts and Coronets", arguably the best film ever made, and "Star Wars", the one with the most Wookies, Alec Guinness won an Oscar in 1957 for best actor in "Bridge Over the River Kwai". As the commander of his fellow Allied prisoners, Colonel Nicholson is tasked with erecting a structure that will support the Japanese war effort. Committed to his strict sense of duty, Guinness's character exacts discipline from his men. What the Japanese guards were unable to effect with punishments and coercion, Guinness is able to produce with order and proper chain of command.

In short, his insistence on proper protocol allows him to commit egregious treason. He has helped the enemy, in wartime, to complete the bridge that will allow the movement of their troops to engage allied forces. Nicholson goes so far as to attempt to thwart a guerrilla action by British soldiers hoping to blow up the bridge. Nicholson's adherence to order allows him to lose sight of the larger picture—helping the enemy in wartime. When he finally comes to grips with what he has done, he exclaims "Madness!"

Speaking of madness, what is the purpose of homework in your house? Is homework about learning, about reinforcing the inspiring lessons that the children have been exposed to in the classroom earlier in the day? Is homework about cuddling up on the couch with your child and a dog-eared copy of <u>Old Yeller</u>? Is homework about falling in love with words and ideas? Is homework about learning?

Or is homework in your house about doing what you're told? Has homework descended into an incessant series of psychotic screaming power and control matches that just don't make any sense to anyone?

Exhausted Mother: Do your homework!

Fatigued Child: Feh!

These altercations remind me of an unfortunate series of Junior High jokes of which the following, regrettably, is not even close to the most egregious example.

Child: Mommy, Mommy, I don't want to go to Europe.

Mother: Shut up and keep swimming!

"But there are responsibilities in the broader world" loving parents opine. "At some point a superior is going to require that responsibilities be fulfilled. Shouldn't my child practice attending to commitments? How can she learn to be accountable as an adult if she doesn't do homework in the third grade?"

Your child may learn to be responsible as an adult. But whether or not she does has very little to do with what you force her to do at age nine. That children may be exposed to carcinogens when they grow up is a poor argument for family vacations at Fukushima Daiichi. If children are forced to do homework, what they may learn is, well, er, force. Of course you may also instill resentment, unhappiness, and a deep seated sense that a parent's function is to badger rather than support.

Remember children learn what they live. Here's my favorite example of a mother correcting her three-year-old who has just smacked a playmate.

"Samantha! (Mom smacks Samantha.) Don't hit!" (SMACK!) "In this family, we U-S-E," (SMACK!) "O-U-R" (SMACK!) "W-O-R-D-S!" (SMACK!) "We don't hit!"

Extra credit if you can tell me whether or not Samantha grew up to be a hitter. Let me not always see the same hands.

Mind you I'm not talking about kids who CAN do the mind numbing, soul denying, insipid worksheets. For kids whose fine motor skills are advanced (read: can write quickly and efficiently) homework will only inhibit their sense of wonder and their love of learning rather than cause shouting matches. But for kids who have trouble getting the words out of their brains and onto the paper, homework struggles can be as lengthy as they are fruitless.

The Forgotten Door by Alexander Key was my favorite book in fifth grade although I hear the Harry Potter series is well written and attractive to young readers as well. A Wrinkle in Time, The Giver, The Hobbit, The Hitchhiker's Guide to the Galaxy, and The Princess Bride are all great reads as are books by John Green and Judy Bloom.

I know a lot of kids who love reading. I don't know hardly any kids who love homework.

Do you have the nerve to take a day off from the homework struggle? Can you put off the assignments and put down the electronics for a marathon weekend of reading? Can you communicate to your kids that in your family words, books, and ideas are what you value rather than worksheets? Can you cuddle up on the couch with your kids and spend hour after hour taking turns reading Frindle or Island of the Blue Dolphins out loud to one another?

Or will you continue to be caught up in the madness?

33

Parenting Quiz

Question One: Your five-year-old daughter comes home from kindergarten with a paper that the children have worked on in class, writing letters and distinguishing shapes or colors.

Your daughter's page does not contain a sticker, although you have noticed that most papers that come home from school do have a "good job" or "nicely done" smiley face sticker attached. Which of the following best describes your reactions and subsequent actions?

A) You cuddle up on the couch with your daughter and some vegetable snacks. You read Robert Lopshire's classic <u>Put Me in the Zoo</u>, arguably the greatest children's book ever written. Then you and your daughter make oatmeal raisin cookies emphasizing that three teaspoons is one table spoon so two table spoons must be six teaspoons.

B) You send an angry text to your child's teacher decrying her blatant discrimination and gross incompetence. Unable to reach her immediately, you send a scathing email to the principal of the elementary school excoriating her for hiring such a person. Excerpts from your repeated texts and emails contain the phrases, "my daughter's self-esteem will be irrevocably harmed" and "all the other children got stickers."

If you picked "A" above, you are my kind of parent. You are allowing your daughter to make her own way. You are not forcing your own anxiety about the future to get in the way of her processing her own experience. If you even noticed that there wasn't a silly sticker on her paper, you set the ground work for her being able to deal with little bumps on her own now so that she'll be able to cope with bigger bumps down the road.

If you picked "B" above, you are, in my professional judgment, careening toward trouble. The time to intervene in your child's kindergarten classroom is when you feel that she is in genuine danger. It's a great idea to allow your child to understand that she can solve problems on her own—IF she even feels that they are problems.

The other reason that I have concerns about choice "B" is that children tend to absorb the anxiety of their parents. We want to communicate to our little ones that the world is basically a safe, protected place. Also, we want to keep our opinions to ourselves about a great many topics. I know wonderful parents with content, high functioning children who used only two words in bringing up their kids. "Drugs and condoms" they said. "We're against the former and—if and when the time comes—in favor of the later." Any other issues—whether or not the child came home with a sticker, for example— they assiduously ignored, preferring that the children make their own way, figure things out on their own.

My last (I promise!) issue with the mother who hovers like a lawn mower over her child's kindergarten classroom is that the behavior makes good teaching that much harder. It's one thing to get a herd of five-year-olds to and from the lunch room and engage them in learning their numbers and letters. It's another level of stress for a teacher to have to be concerned about an overbearing mom looking over her shoulder, second guessing her every curricular choice.

Some of the worst teaching that is done at the elementary level results from teachers who are worried about how parents will react. Norm referenced testing which is contraindicated for all children but especially visceral for little ones is a result of those crazy parents who won't leave the kindergarten teacher alone and let her do her job. "I can't explain about 'ages and stages'" teachers lament. "The parents don't get it when I talk about how not every child is ready to read at age five. So I administer those harmful tests. At least I can show the parents percentiles and graphs. Then they leave me alone. For a few days."

Oh, and what happened to the missing sticker, the sticker that caused the outraged mom to write the scathing emails? The sticker was "found" on the child's desk at school. The child had pulled the sticker off of her paper and put in on her desk.

Problem solved; but another set of more intractable problems created.

34

Boodleheimer

My best friends growing up were three brothers who introduced me to—among other things—<u>The Silly Book</u>, and the cartoon character, "Boodleheimer." It would be difficult, almost 50 years down the road, to overestimate the extraordinary joy that Rod, Paul, Frank, and I got from the following verse of the "Silly Song":

Boodleheimer
Boodleheimer

(CLAP! CLAP! CLAP!)

Boodleheimer
Boodleheimer

(CLAP! CLAP! CLAP!)

The more you Boodle,
The less you Heimer.
The more you Heimer,
The less you Boodle.

Boodleheimer
Boodleheimer

(CLAP! CLAP! CLAP!)

Even now as I write this, an adult man with grown children, I can barely
contain my joy. And is those days, we couldn't get past the first "Boodle"
without breaking out in breathless tears. And the capital letters in "CLAP!"
And all those exclamation points! This was the early sixties, remember. The
starchy Eisenhower presidency was only one administration in the past. A
profligate profusion of exclamation points was not to be overlooked.

The 50s were not silly. Boodleheimer presaged the raucous 60s. Our fifth
grade selves seemed to sense that something was coming down the pike. If
Dick and Jane had been replaced by "boodle" and "heimer," could the
Smothers Brothers, tie-dye, and love-ins be far behind?

It would take us 20 gasping minutes to thoroughly engulf the unmitigated
hilarity—the Boodleheimer appeared on subsequent pages as well—before
going outside to toss a coconut at one other and then returning to read The
Silly Book once again. It's a wonder we stopped long enough to eat lunch or
pay attention to the Gemini space missions.

***

Ron, Paul, and Frank lost their parents when they were young men and my
dad, the attorney for their dad, was put in charge of their money—"estate"
would be too grand a word. My dad cheerfully doled out checks for college
tuition, acting in accordance with the wishes of my friends's dad, a man
whom he had known most of his life. It was simple and straightforward for
my dad to decide what to fund. There was enough money for undergraduate
education and, if interest rates remained high, most of law school for all three
boys.

Unfortunately, Frank lost his way and became heavily involved with drugs.
Bordering on destitute, he showed up at my dad's office demanding money.

My father was equally determined not to squander Frank's small inheritance and refused to give him a nickel until and unless he was clean. Their talk began badly and deteriorated quickly:

Frank: "Uncle Richard, it's my money. My dad left it for me. I can do what I want with it."

My Dad, (all 5' 7" of him): "Then come get it."

Needless to say, Frank was not in a position to litigate and he wouldn't have gotten any money if he had. My dad had the moral high ground as well as the law on his side. Frank did get clean though and, of course, my dad funded his education all the way through law school. The money from Frank's dad ran out along the way, but my dad kept writing checks. What was he going to do? Frank was the youngest son of his good friend, now free of drugs and in law school.

Fast forward ten years. My dad has long since forgotten the unpleasantness of his conversations with Frank during the time when Frank was using. They exchange cards now and again. My dad is pleased to hear of Frank's continued sobriety and incipient law practice. One day Frank shows up in my dad's office. After the traditional exchange of pleasantries, Frank tosses my dad a wad of twenty dollars bills with which you could choke a horse. My dad, feigning ignorance, said, "What's this?"

Frank said, "I'm not stupid, Uncle Richard. I know how much money my dad left me. I know where the money for my tuition came from."

***

So now the question becomes: should my dad accept the money—several thousand dollars. I'm going to argue that he should. Not just because the money was his, but because Frank needed to pay it back. Sometimes, you just have to accept a gift.

What does this story—admittedly one of my favorites—have to do with being good parents? Ignoring the obvious, that having stand up morals is healthy for kids, what about the idea of accepting gifts? Too often parents play the part of martyrs. "Look how I suffer," they intone. "Look how much I pay for your private school, the sacrifices I make. And you won't even take out the garbage or put your dirty plate in the dishwasher." This syllogism is untenable. Bad reasoning leads to children who don't understand the value of being part of something larger than themselves. Children must be allowed to make a contribution to the running of the household. Not every child can learn calculus, but any child without significant physical limitations can and should be expected to take the trash buckets out to the street on Monday and Thursday mornings.

After which they should be welcome to come back inside and read <u>The Silly Book</u> to their heart's content.

35

Dog in Fight

The temperature in the high 80s with 100% humidity at mile 20 of a recent marathon, my friend Daniel glanced down as we stumbled by a line of broken, twitching bodies writhing on the side of the road, runners unable to continue. We weren't in significantly better shape ourselves—pasty, salty skin, achy and beyond miserable—but we were still plodding forward. Ambulance after ambulance whizzed by to aid dehydrated, dazed runners. I tried not to think about that scene from "Gone with the Wind." You know: the one with all the injured soldiers.

"Ah." Daniel remarked. "The race begins now."

In college admissions, families seem more and more focused on "getting in" than on what the kids can do in the classroom if they do get admitted. Donating five hundred thousand dollars to the development fund and blackmailing the dean of admissions might be useful strategies—they're not; but it's fun to think that they could be—but what happens when Percy is asked to write an actual in-class essay or to solve a calculus problem? A castle built on sand sinks pretty quickly when the tide comes in. And finding the volume of a three-dimensional solid as it expands while hurtling through space requires the reality rather than the appearance of ability.

"But 98 % of the graduates of VCU ("Vine Covered University" for the purposes of this example, rather than Virginia Commonwealth) are admitted to law school." Yes, because of who the kids were when they started, not because of what VCU did for them once they matriculated.

"Are you sure that what you do is more important than where you go?"

Yes, I'm sure. Having skill, learning a lot, and doing well at No Name U allows you to go to graduate school and do well when you're there. Matriculating at Single Digit Admission Rate College and not being able to handle what goes on in the classroom leaves you wishing for a paddle.

If "Going to church doesn't make you a Christian any more than sleeping in the garage makes you a car" then attending VCU won't transform a student of modest ability into an able practitioner any more than putting this author in a Miami Dolphins uniform will allow me to make any actual tackles.

It's not about getting in, it's about connecting and making progress once you're there.

As my 12th grade clients finalize their selections, I ask them to look beyond the hype and to focus on what goes on in the typical classroom on a typical college day. Does the teaching style in the classroom match the learning style of the student?

Of course other factors of all kinds come into the calculus of making a decision about which school to attend. I would never decry the value of a football game, an outing with the hiking club, an opportunity to make a contribution to the student newspaper or radio station. But at some point, the number of October classics in which Vine Covered University emerged victorious will matter less that whether or not its graduates can pose, research, solve, and articulate the answers to sophisticated questions.

No potential employer ever differentiated among applicants based on college hockey game attendance. No graduate school dean ever decided to grant admission based on how many formal dances were attended. The match between the quality of the undergraduate teaching and the way students learn is the critical piece. And the better the student is at learning the better.

First year biology at this university is the same as first year biology at that university is as true as suggesting that all spouses are equally good matches. (Ask anyone who has ever been married more than once about the truth of the later statement.) What happens in the classroom is what matters. It doesn't matter where you get in if you can't stay in.

I have written repeatedly about how competition is harmful for developing minds. Focusing on performance takes away from attending to learning. That said, you have to know whom you're sitting next to at We Have Higher SAT Scores University. That kid in the front row using his phone, the one you think is texting his girlfriend? He's not texting anyone. He's using his phone to record the lecture. He asked permission of the professor when you were at the pep rally. That kid listens to the recorded lectures—sometimes more than once—while he fills in any notes he may have missed during class. Sometimes he transcribes the lectures word for word.

Sometimes he memorizes the lectures. Memorizes. As if he were an actor in a play.

Can you imagine how well that kid does on the exams? Every test he takes is "open book" because he has memorized all the lectures word for word. He doesn't just know the material. He knows everything in the professor's head. Yes, he studies hard. For all we know he may even miss the occasional sporting event because he's in the library. He makes use of office hours; he gets together with friends to study; he is immaculately organized. He gets the job done.

He is just like the Terminator. Only more focused.

If you go to Single Digit Admission Rate College or We Have Higher SAT Scores University, you better be ready to go toe to toe with this kid. Because that's where he goes to school and you better have the skill and the motivation to stay with him. At 20 miles out, when everyone else is cramping and barfing, when the other runners are dazed and staggering, this kid is picking up the pace, running through the paramedics, studying like a machine, memorizing lectures, learning everything.

And he's sitting next to you, studying the same coursework, doing the same labs, taking the same exams.

Wouldn't you agree that being <u>admitted</u> to Single Digit Admissions Rate College or We Have Higher SAT Scores University is the least of your worries?

36

Upstairs Craig and the $15 Loan

My undergraduate roommate, Joel, and I had become fairly friendly with our upstairs neighbor in our off-campus apartment junior year. I don't know about Joel, but I thought it was fun to have an acquaintance who had a real job. Everyone else we knew was a student. Craig seemed much more of a grownup. Passing on the stairs, Joel and I would complain about problem sets in our "Non-Euclidean Geometry and Convexity" and five-page papers for our "Hawthorne, Twain, and Melville" courses. Craig would complain about his low paying job.

We were hardly surprised thereby, when Craig knocked on our door one Tuesday afternoon. After the obligatory pleasantries—Joel and I had an exam coming up; Craig was annoyed with his boss—Craig talked about his financial situation: it was dire. Craig owed money to a number of his friends, he was behind on his rent and—this is why he had come downstairs to talk to us—the electric company was going to turn off his power if he didn't get over to their office with a payment within the next two hours.

He needed $15.

It is perhaps noteworthy to put the dollars in context. Minimum wage was $1.60 an hour in 1976. Fifteen dollars therefore represented a little more money than Joel or I could earn in a full day of work grading math papers. Fifteen dollars was also a little less than what it cost to feed us for a full week. A pound of hamburger or a pound of cheese were both about a dollar and a half. I'm no economist, but I think $15 in my college days would be about $150 today.

Craig swore up and down that he would pay Joel back on Friday, that he only needed the money for three days, that he was going to get paid and would give Joel the $15 first thing after work on Friday afternoon. I remember the phrase "You have my word as a friend" being repeated.

Joel loaned Craig the $15. Needless to say, Craig used the money to buy a keg of beer and have some friends over. It is now 37 years later and I think it is safe to assume that Craig will not pay back the $15 that he owes to Joel.

My buddy, Joel, is now long since out of law school, has three grown children, and is coming up on his fourth decade of marriage to "the girl of his dreams." Though far apart geographically, Joel and I still chat a couple of times each year. The subject of "Upstairs Craig and the $15 Loan" comes up now and again.

For years and years the message of this story was, "How could we have been so dumb?" Of course, Craig was the worst of bad credit risks. He already owed money to everybody he knew. We should have known he had no intention—certainly no ability—to pay back the $15.

Over time though, the subtext has evolved. Now when we talk about Craig and the $15 loan, Joel and I have a different view. Joel is still the same sweet guy he was in the mid-70s, generous to a fault. But he is in a different financial position. He is now a successful attorney in New York, not a starving college student taking public transportation to the grocery store trying to feed himself on under ten bucks a week. Joel now gets asked for loans or all kinds, loans in the $15,000 to $150,000 range.(Sometimes these loans are disguised as "opportunities" to purchase stock.)

As a result of Craig's thoughtful lesson imparted all those years ago, Joel is better able to discern a good credit risk from a young man who is likely to invest in beer.

What's the take away for loving parents trying to bring up healthy kids in this unhealthy world? It's hard to argue for allowing our children to use bad judgment. It's hard to lecture to a room full of concerned adults about allowing our children to fail. Yet it is the small failures when they are young that inoculate against the larger failures later.

"But if I don't do his homework for him then he'll fall behind and he won't get into a good college" opines the mother of a ninth grader. To which a response might be, "Honey, if you're doing homework for a 15-year-old, admission to a good college is the least of your worries."

Most alcoholics have an enabler in their past, someone who softened the blow, rescued them from suffering the consequences of their actions. We can't force our children to be successful in school any more than we can force the alcoholics in our lives to stop drinking. What we can do is allow them to find their own way to success.

This unattractive lesson for parents might be stated as: The less you do for your children, the more they will be able to do for themselves. Or, our children can't learn from their mistakes if we never allow them to make any.

37

Sit Down

Look, I'm just going to come right out and say it: Telling your child that she should work hard so that she can be Number One is just stupid.

Because, by definition, only one person can be first. It's arithmetic. As easy as—forgive me—one, two three. If your child is first, then somebody else's child isn't. That's all there is to it.

Having your child focus on being Number One is stupid, damaging, harmful, and demeaning. Because if she fails to achieve Number One-ness, then she has failed in the eyes of her parents. And if she does make it to Number One-ville, then she has learned to treat her classmates as objects.

I went to a Dolphin's game the other day. I was sitting comfortably in my chair enjoying my unobstructed view of the contest when the man in front of me stood up to get a better look at the field. Not his fault—he stood up because the person in front of him had stood up. You can see where this is going. In less than a New York Minute, every soul in my section of the stadium was on his or her feet. Where we had all been fine before, ensconced on our tushies and able to see just fine, now we all had to stand in order to see. If everyone sits, we can all see just as well as if everyone stands. Of course if everyone stands, everyone's feet hurt. If I wanted my feet to hurt, I would have gone for a run instead of purchasing a ticket to a football game.

Consider the SAT, which used to be known as the Scholastic Aptitude Test. To keep the arithmetic simple, I'll talk about the math section. The math section of the SAT has an average score of 500 and the results are "normally distributed." (You don't have to know what "normally distributed" means to understand every word of this essay.) For every child who scores a 510—10 points above the average—there's another child who scores 10 points below the average. For every child who scores a 600, there's another child who scores a 400. Think about it: could every child score an 800, the highest score? No. The test would be useless. No student would pay $43 to take the test. No family would pay $11 to send their child's scores to a college. No college would pay money to be on the College Board. "Oh, look," an admissions officer would say. "This applicant ALSO has an 800 on the SAT Math." On a norm referenced test like the SAT Math, if there is no variance, then there is no score.

As the test exists now, the only way your child can get an 800 is if someone else's child gets a 200. In other words, it may be possible to raise the score of one child on the SAT Math, but it is not possible to raise the score of ALL children on the SAT Math.

Think about a "selfless" coach who works with an economically disadvantaged athlete from a third world country preparing the young man for big time baseball. Hour after hour, the dedicated mentor works on hitting, fielding, throwing and catching. Tirelessly, the coach helps prepare his young charge for every aspect of the competition to come, driving him to away games, teaching him strategy. And then, the great day comes, and the low income kid gets his chance in the show. And he gets a million dollar contract! And he does an after shave commercial! And he gives lectures to other low income young men about how they too can make it! That's great, right? The coach has done a good thing! The alternative for this young man from the lousy neighborhood would have been a life of privation and hardship!

True, this young man now has a life.

But some other young man doesn't.

Because there are still only 30 major league baseball teams with extended rosters of 40 players each. The patient coach didn't invent another million dollars for his protege. In a very real sense, he stole that million dollars from some other hard working prospect.

***

Stacey is not just a substance abuser or an addict, she has become chemically dependent. Having put her last thousand dollars up her nose, she desperately needs and is ready to accept treatment. But all the programs that take her insurance are full with waiting lists of over six months.

Through my contacts in the drug rehab community, I am able to move her to the "head of the line" and get her into a quality program. I've done a good thing, right? There should be a parade in my honor, no? I have helped Stacey get a chance to kick the debilitating habit that is destroying her life and the lives of all those who care about her.

Nah. All I've done is keep some other poor deserving soul from getting the treatment that she too so desperately requires.

***

My child is "Student of the Month!" Great!

Nah. My daughter's "victory" just means that there are 23 other precious children in that kindergarten class who are NOT student of the month.

And don't even get me started on those folks who want to put my website at the top of the search engines. Did we learn nothing from the Cold War?

What if it were possible for me to help your child become, say, the Number One Professor at Yale Law School? Heck, I'd be happy for your child, I can't deny it. But somewhere, someone else's child, would learn that she is not going to be that Number One bulldog (the Yale mascot.)

In a very real sense, emphasizing that your child be Number One is like suggesting that your child be the only one to stand at the Dolphin game. It's not going to happen, not to more than one child anyway.

But everyone else is hiring tutors, looking for every advantage, trying to get the extra edge in admissions and in life; I would be a fool not to. Don't misunderstand. I'm in favor of kids working hard, trying to be the best they can be. But taking unfair advantage to take the one Number One spot ruins the game for everyone. Ask Lance Armstrong. If you can get that lying, bullying, cheating drug crazed, psycho creep to return your call.

What's the answer? How do we help our kids be healthy in a crazed, broken system of competitive sports and competitive classrooms? By helping our children to be the smartest, most compassionate, most well read, most able, most studious, most helpful, most pleasant children that they can be. By encouraging them to ignore everyone else. The competition isn't the Visigoths come to plunder your village; the "competition" is someone else's beloved child.

.

38

It's Only a Game?

My limited understanding of the mortgage debacle was that there were "bunches" of bundled debts, some of which were supposed to be "good" mortgages and some of which were understood to be "not so good" mortgages. Shockingly, it turned out that each and every one of the mortgages in the tranches completely, uniformly, and without exception belonged to the latter "not so good" category. I believe, the sophisticated financial term used to describe these collections of mortgages was "horrible." Every one of the $250,000 mortgages was secured by a leaky trailer valued at dozens of dollars. Sometimes the same trailer.

Not that any American tax payer should have been surprised. At every Publix are gumball machines where the prizes that a whining child can "see" differ significantly from the crap that the crying child can "receive" after wheedling a quarter from a grocery laden parent. Similarly, there is a picture of an eighty thousand dollar car in the casino. If you put quarters in a slot machine long enough, you might win that car! The photograph of a man returning home without groceries to his hungry family because he has put all his quarters in a machine and has—once again—not won a car?

That photo is not displayed.

The assumption that I make when I see a family eating high calorie, low nutrition fast food is that this meal is the exception, that most meals are prepared with healthy ingredients in a pleasant home. The reality, of course, is that many families eat McDreck from a drive through more often than they steam vegetables in their kitchen.

Surely, there is nothing wrong with the occasional family gathering around the television to view a favorite show. But when screens become the norm and conversation the exception, something has gone horribly awry.

The first time I heard "if you take away my game, I'll kill myself" was just under ten years ago. The 16-year-old speaker wasn't kidding, although he may have been exaggerating. I now hear "if you take away my video game, I'll kill myself" from 13 year olds. Recently, I heard "if you take away my video game, I'll kill myself" from a ten-year-old.

For these kids—younger and younger each year—playing "Shoot, Blood, Kill" isn't the rare half hour after a full day of reading, bike riding, and exploring wild places with friends. Snorting X-Box is two or three hours every day, more—much more—on weekends. Other activities, especially those involving interaction with other actual humans, have been curtailed severely.

How are ten-year-olds becoming addicts? (Such an ugly word, but the accurate one.) For one thing, game designers are making the games "stickier" with every edition. The NSA has nothing on game designers. "After the kid found the gold in the castle, he played for two more hours;" "after the unicorn died, the kid stopped playing" is exactly the data that is collected, analyzed, and implemented to keep your child's dopamine receptors buzzing and your child connected (pun intended) to the multi-player on-line game.

Those who profit from your children injecting on-line games hide behind the "we only provide entertainment for those who choose to play" argument the way cigarette manufacturers claim that they only provide tar and nicotine for those who have already chosen to smoke. These contentions would be laughable if they weren't so heinous. We've all heard a bartender say, "Don't you think you've had enough?" Has anyone from a tobacco company ever said, "I don't think you should have another cigarette"? Has any game designer ever suggested, "You've played enough 'Shoot, Blood, Kill'"?

It has often been remarked that the best way to stop is not to start, that it's easier to stay out of trouble that to get out of trouble. Parents can easily "just say no" to addictive computer games when the kids are little. It's another kettle of electrons altogether when the children are older. Here's another way to conceptualize pulling the plug on video games when you still have influence: "Pay me now or pay me later."

Now is cheaper.

Admittedly, gaming addiction has more in common with eating disorders than it does with addiction to cigarettes, alcohol, drugs, or gambling. A heroin abuser in recovery can live a happy, healthy life if she never shoots up again. (Indeed, it can be argued that a heroin abuser in recovery can live a happy, healthy life ONLY if she never shoots up again.) For an alcoholic, "one is too many and a hundred isn't enough." But a young adult with an eating disorder cannot say, "I'll never eat again." A healthy relationship with food is necessary for survival. Similarly, a child who has an unhealthy relationship with computer gaming cannot avoid screens completely. Internet research and word processing are necessary for school survival. The tricky bit is to stay focused on homework and to avoid checking email or playing "Shoot, Blood, Kill" "just for a few minutes."

The best time to plant an oak tree was 20 years ago; the second best time to plant an oak tree is today.

The best time to start the "no computer games" policy in your home was when you brought the kids home from the maternity ward.

The second best time to throw away all your screens is today.

39

The Sorting Hat

That organic chemistry makes more sociology majors than it does doctors is well known. Less obvious, is that colleges who claim that "92% of our premedical students are admitted to medical school!" are not revealing the entire stethoscope. The 92 % admission figure may be accurate, but what happened to those bright eyed first-year students who weren't counted, the ones who "changed their minds" about studying medicine? Had they applied to medical school-with their B- averages, they would not have been among the 92%. Medical schools look beyond A students as often as the NBA plays sub-six footers. It happens; but don't mortgage the farm.

The other admissions issue, of course, is who the successful applicants were to begin with. Brilliant, motivated, emotionally intelligent 18 year-olds with immaculate study skills have a greater likelihood of ending up in operating rooms just as they previously had a predilection for appearing in "top" colleges. To hint that their (admittedly wonderful) undergraduate educations are completely responsible for these kids running the O.R. is akin to believing that incarceration is what causes released prisoners to be unable to land jobs as CEOs. The fact is that those college students had everything on the ball to begin with. As the felons, unfortunately, did not.

What intrigues me lately is how far back the sorting process goes. As middle-schoolers, Harry, Ron, and Hermione all end up in Gryffindor. No muggles allowed. My colleagues in admissions have had the luxury of denying those applicants who "wouldn't fit it," a euphemism for kids who don't have the horses, ever since pre-school.

It is no wonder parents don't laugh at my observation regarding an "APGAR preparation seminar." It is no surprise that expectant parents play music for their developing embryos. Alcohol harms fetuses, anxious parents argue, shouldn't music help them? (Answer: no, playing music to your unborn progeny does not make a difference post-partum. Anyone who tells you differently is trying to sell you something.)

Admissions officers at expensive private elementary schools have had the luxury of picking the most likely to succeed from among baskets of lovely five-year-olds. The best of the admitted cherubs who dodge the odd pitfall—video game and drug addiction, overbearing parents—subsequently trot off toward their surgical residencies.

The change that's coming for private schools is in demographics and economics. Only a few selective schools at any level are going to remain unravaged by the reality that private day schools and boarding schools used to be affordable for a larger percentage of families. Unlike colleges, where comfortable endowments allow young people from modest backgrounds to attend, boarding schools are more reliant on tuition. Previously, private day and traditional boarding school could focus on educating strong students from families who could write checks. Now the mission statements of these schools are being rewritten to include phrases such as "environment that celebrates acceptance," "each student's success," and "holistic approach." That's a long way from "superior academics," "scholarly excellence," and "competitive sports teams."

Colleges are changing their marketing as well. Schools whose admissions offices used to send a catalog replete with course descriptions of differential equations and Advanced Sanskrit are now replacing courses in Neurophysiology with—in Gary Trudeau's wonderful description—"Our Friend the Beaver." Admission brochures of 40 years ago, stern black and white affairs emphasizing academic rigor have been replaced with websites bursting with videos of exuberant students beaming at sporting events and social activities.

Needless to say, this author is wildly in favor of schools meeting students where they are and helping them to achieve more than they ever thought possible. A 2:30 marathoner focuses or running 2:20. A 4:30 marathoner devotes his training to achieving 4:20. It's when the 4:30 finisher tries to run 2:20 that knees explode and paramedics arrive with bags of I.V. glucose. When parents force their kids who could benefit from attending "supported to achieve their academic best" into "demanding academics" that sadness follows.

"No matter where you go, there you are" is a telling psychological insight. Allowing your kids to be content with who they are, as my long suffering readers know, is my favorite prescription for happy families—where ever the sorting hat puts them.

40

Do You Need a Date?

Some years ago driving to my girlfriend's house, I saw an attractive young woman hitch hiking. Concerned about the quality of the neighborhood and eager to offer a hand, I slowed to a stop. This was the late 70s and girls with their thumbs out were rare. I pulled over and stood up between the driver's seat and the door of my car. "Do you need a ride?" I asked.

From the sidewalk, the appealing young woman replied, "Do you need a date?"

Admittedly, a Martian who had been observing Earth culture for 20 minutes would have been able to perceive the occupation of the young woman with whom I was now conversing obliviously, but I blathered on. "No, I don't want a date," I said, puzzled. "I'm on my way to my girlfriend's house just now as it happens and we were going to see if there are any movies playing although a couple weeks ago we saw this film that I kinda liked but she thought that the cinematography was overrated, but I'm sure she wouldn't mind if I were a few minutes late if I dropped you somewhere because this neighborhood these past few years has..."

It was only then that the proverbial penny dropped and rattled around in my cerebral cortex and I was able to discern what all the pieces—the impossibly short shorts, the shining fingernails, the halter top, the incredulous attitude—added up to.

Immediately unable to form a coherent thought never mind speak, I slid back into my car and sped off. Yes, I was indeed having a conversation about my aesthetic perception of 20th century cinema with a prostitute. No, I'm not proud of it.

My point here is not to make fun of my naive twenty-something year old self—indeed, that target is too large to present a significant challenge—but to pose two related questions: 1) How different could my life have been had this conversation been observed by someone other than the two participants? 2) Was I in need of an intervention of some kind?

First off, let's try to imagine the dubious musings by a savvy police officer.

"Mr. Altshuler, let's go over this again."

"Yes, sir."

"You say that the woman was wearing clothing that looked like it was painted on?"

"Yes, sir."

"You say that you knew the temperature was 50 degrees?

"Yes, sir."

"And you say the woman asked you if you wanted a date?"

"Yes, sir."

"But you say that you didn't know that she was a prostitute?"

"No, sir."

***

Now to the second point—when to intervene: When our adolescent children do something so incredibly immature, when our kids do something so mind numbingly ill advised, when our kids commit an act so egregiously lacking in common sense that we stand slack jawed in awe, glassy-eyed in disbelief that we had anything to do with the conception and upbringing of this person who is saying, "It wasn't me," how do we proceed?

Because in actuality, beyond a shadow of a doubt reasonable or otherwise, it was you. How do I know it was you? Because there's no one else in the room. That's how I know. And before I walked in here a moment ago and turned my back, I am thoroughly certain that your eviscerated stuffed animal was not attached to the ceiling fan.

So now the question becomes, "one and done" versus "teachable moment." The 15 year-old with marijuana that "isn't his" in his backpack who just got kicked out of school? Again? Actually, that marijuana is his. And this issue needs to be addressed. When does this issue need to be addressed? Does *yesterday* work for you?

But the kid who sneaks out in the middle of the night to go for a walk with her friends? Maybe she is telling the truth when she says she just wanted to see what the stars looked like just before the sun comes up.

Loving parents must, as always, walk the middle path and find moderation. It's naive not to be concerned about an adolescent who smokes pot, runs away, and gets kicked out of school; on the other hand, it's over-the-top anxious to worry every minute about a kid who ignores an occasional homework assignment or stays up late reading a book with a flashlight under the covers.

Even Freud wrote that "sometimes a cigar is just a cigar." Sometimes even the most improbable statements are true; sometimes the most likely utterances are not.

Or as Thurber said in "The Bear Who Let it Alone," "You might as well fall flat on your face as lean over too far backward." Making the tough calls, determining when to jump in and when to let kids figure things out for themselves, is what good parenting is all about.

145

41

Sex Ed, Advice, Schnauzers

In a sex ed class some 40 years ago, a student whom I did not know well asked a question about reproductive biology. His inquiry, something specific about condoms as I recall, impressed me as highly theoretical at the time. It is certainly possible that he was honestly requesting information about how to avoid pregnancy. It was not until many years later that his actual agenda occurred to me: he was bragging.

Which is fine. I certainly do not begrudge my high school contemporary his opportunity to proclaim to his classmates that he was sexually active. But what are we to make of our fellow parents of high school age children who ask questions about the academic progress of my children? "How many AP classes is your daughter taking?" begins a seemingly well intentioned mom whom I hardly know in the high school parking lot. Before I can begin to formulate an answer of the form "and that would be your business because..." the invariable onslaught continues. "You know, my daughter is taking six AP classes this year. We talked about whether or not she should take a seventh advance placement course but we didn't want to pressure her." Again, before I can sputter, "how could you possibly imagine that I would be interested in your daughter's curriculum?" she goes on to say that college admissions officers want to see the most sophisticated academic coursework that the high school has to offer and that her child will be applying to Princeton and Stanford with Duke as a safety and that last year three students from the school were accepted at Cornell but that this year the class is stronger although the coach of the soccer team doesn't let her daughter to score as many goals as she should...

And on and on.

Having listened to parents describe their children the way a proud farmer might brag about the amount of milk produced by a prized cow, I have frequently refrained from asking these moms if they would like a bumper sticker. Something of the form, "I have a schnauzer" might be nice.

Because as far as her advice goes about how many AP classes my child should take, I feel pretty strongly about "No thank you." Indeed, I might go so far as to say, "How dare you?" Because you're not actually giving me advice about my child; you're just bragging about yours.

The fact is, this other parent doesn't know me. She certainly doesn't know my child. She's never been to my house for dinner. (There's a reason for that.) She doesn't know the first thing about me. Yet she tells me how many advanced placement classes my daughter should take. What if my child were developmentally disabled? What if my child had an IQ of 60? What if my child were unable to take college-level classes never mind advanced ones? Yet somehow this mother has the unmitigated temerity to give me advice that pertains, arguably, to *her* child.

Another irony, of course, is that she doesn't have the first idea how college admissions to top colleges actually works, nor does she know the first thing about good parenting. She relies on a few rumors and some anecdotal evidence about some other kid who was admitted to a highly competitive university a generation ago and as a result she presumes to give me advice about how my child could be admitted to a college that would be completely wrong for her.

Her logic is as offensive as it is inaccurate.

Her first point—that my child must take the most sophisticated academic coursework her high school has to offer in order to be admitted to a highly competitive school—is mostly accurate. While it is true that students in the entering class at Stanford had many advanced classes, it is also true that 69% of students with a dozen AP classes AND 2400 on the SAT were denied admission. So her hypothesis that taking advanced classes will result in admission at a highly competitive school is absurd. Advanced classes are a necessary but not sufficient condition.

Her next point that my child should take certain coursework and rush down the road to nowhere is offensive.

Her twisted, soul denying, ridiculous ideas about how to bring up her child are up to her.

Leave me out of it.

I like my kids just the way they are, thank you just the same. No matter how many AP classes they take, no matter where they end up going to college.

42

Trick Question

Which of the following first person stories seems more plausible?

1) "There were these two sets of double doors between the dining room and the kitchen. I carried trays stacked high with the leftover food from the plates of the patrons. On the way to hand the trays to the dishwasher, I had three steps, about two seconds. With good balance and a little luck, I could inhale a quick mouthful of half-eaten food."

"Disgusting? Maybe. Unsafe? Probably. But the food was great and the alternative was hunger. Sometimes people would hardly touch their meals and I could scarf down half a hamburger or a handful of French fries. For two years, the best food I ate was during those trips to the kitchen."

"My mom left when I was 16, took off to California to be with her boyfriend, a used car salesman. She said she's send money every month, but I wasn't surprised when she never did. I missed some meals, sure, but I was lucky to get that job at the Eden Roc, busing tables. My dad had disappeared years before. I don't have any memories of him. There was no social safety net in those days; there were no family members who could take me in. So I finished high school and got another job that got me through college. I spent a year in the service then went to medical school. Of course, I always worked. Sure, I was hungry most of the time and tired all of the time. But I made it through."

"Now I have a successful medical practice. I still work half a day on Saturday although I guess I don't really need to. Old habits die hard. My daughters are grown, but they live close by and we have brunch every Sunday. They bring the grandchildren. It's a joy to watch them grow up. I'm glad that I am able to provide for them so that they don't have to work quite as hard as I did. They're good kids. I'm happy for them."

***

2) "My mom is such a bitch. Why is she always waking me up to go to school? School is stupid. I'm not learning anything and the stuff they teach is so useless. If she would just leave me alone and let me play Mindcraft, everything would be okay. It's not like I want to play "Call of Duty" like my friends. That game is addictive and bad. Mindcraft is good for you. I learn more from that game than I would if I paid attention in school.

"And what is up with her sending me to that stupid therapist? What a waste of time. So I smoke a little pot, so what? First of all pot is good for you. It's not addictive like alcohol or cigarettes and all my friends smoke pot anyway. If my therapist tells me to stop smoking pot, I'm not going to go to therapy anymore. And don't even get me started about my stupid tutor. I can't believe my mom is throwing money away on that idiot. Math is such a waste of time. Doesn't he understand that I have a learning disability? I just don't get math and I don't care."

"What's the worst of it? My dad is never around; he works all the time. Which is fine. He's an idiot too like my mom. But I told them that if they'd get me a car for my birthday last month that I wouldn't yell at them when I have friends over. Of course, I reserve the right to call my mom a bitch when we're home alone because she is a bitch. But anyway, they got me this Lexus. And then they told me that I have to get a job to help pay for gas, that they would pay for 99% of the gas, car insurance, and maintenance but that I would have to contribute one percent for the rest. Are they kidding? I'm not going to get some stupid job just so I can pay one percent. I already told them that I'm not good at math; I can't figure out what one percent is. And besides, I don't want a stupid Lexus. I want a BMW. See what I told you? My parents are both so stupid."

***

Which of the monologues above is accurate? Actually, it was a trick question. Actually both of them are close to word for word transcriptions. Without betraying the confidentiality of the speakers, I wrote down every syllable. The only difference is that the doctor quoted in the first set of paragraphs is older that the student speaking in the second set.

For whom would we predict a more content life, the doctor who was given nothing or the young man who has been given everything? Who is more likely to be successful? Who is more likely to feel fulfilled?

Needless to say, I am not advocating for child abandonment and abuse. The doctor's mother behaved despicably, putting her own needs—trotting off to California with her lover—above the needs of her child. Mom should have done what she needed to so that her son could have a place to stay, food to eat, and an easier path through medical school.

But the snarky, spoiled child has been abused too. He will never experience the deeply felt joy that comes from seeing the fruit of his own hard labor; he will never be able to appreciate the peace that comes from knowing he has done the best he could and that he has triumphed against long odds. He will never even learn that working for an hour at nine dollars the hour allows you to buy a sandwich and a drink and have two dollars left over. Simple arithmetic can be a joy.

And a little adversity goes a long way.

43

Stop Me if You've Heard this One

Sparks and smoke billow unabashedly from a dozen places in a 18-ton machine covering 4000 square feet of a factory floor. Gears whine pointlessly as 30 men stand uselessly at their positions along the unmoving conveyor belt. Dozens of trucks are lined up outside, filled with raw materials to be processed by the broken behemoth; dozens more truck wait empty for product that is not being produced.

The boss is distraught. Overhead is killing him; screaming emails, faxes, and phone calls flood in from frantic retail distributors. "My order was supposed to be here three days ago!" "I'm going to take my business elsewhere!" "You promised that your machine would be fixed yesterday!" Meanwhile payroll continues to accrue as crews of experts, the best engineers in the city, fail to get the machine running.

Finally, just as all hope is fading, just as the boss envisions bankruptcy and disgrace, an elderly, wizened man appears on the factory floor. Wiping his dirty hands on his greasy overalls, he stands surveying the havoc. The elderly man looks at the smoke, flame, and sparks; he considers the 30 men standing idly by at their stations at the conveyor belt; he listens to the grinding of the gears. Slowly, he ambles forward toward the massive machine. Approaching a gear box, he opens the panel and takes a Philips Head screw driver from the belt around his hip.

He inserts the screwdriver into one of the screws in the gear box and twists the screw one-quarter turn.

As if by magic, the flames and sparks instantly disappear. The whining gears are immediately silenced as the conveyor belt smoothly begins to run. The workers shout with joy as products are finished and loaded onto the waiting trucks. Within seconds, the factory is once again a productive, profitable place.

The elderly man ambles upstairs to the office of the boss and hands him a grimy piece of paper on which the following words are scrawled in uneven letters:

Bill for services..$10,000

The boss is apoplectic. Sputtering with rage, he gesticulates wildly and screams at the elderly man. "Ten thousand dollars? Ten thousand dollars! This is an outrage! You only worked for two minutes. You can't charge me ten thousand dollars for turning one lousy, little screw."

"I only charged you ten dollars for turning the screw," replies the elderly man.

Even angrier now and confused as well, the boss screams, "What are you talking about? This bill is for ten *thousand* dollars, not ten dollars! What about the other nine thousand something dollars?"

"Ah," says the elderly man with a nod. "The other nine thousand dollars? THAT was for knowing which screw to turn."

***

What can loving parents learn from the elderly man with the greasy overalls and the screw driver? Sometimes it's okay for our kids to struggle the least little bit before giving them the answer. "Wait for the question" the Buddha

153

teaches. A child who is making her own way and discovers for herself that she is stuck on a math problem will be receptive to help. A child who has watched her parents take responsibility for her learning less so.

If getting the homework done has become an unmitigated nightmare in your home replete with flames and sparks shooting out of the machine that should be your well-oiled and smoothly operating family, it might be time to take a step back. Allowing your child to take charge of her own process might just be equivalent to giving that screw a one-quarter turn.

44

Do Your Job Right and You're Unemployed

"I knew a father who had a son,
He longed to tell him all the reasons for the things he'd done.
He came a long way, just to explain.
He kissed his boy as he lay sleeping then he turned around and headed home again."

—Paul Simon, "Slip Slidin' Away," 1977

"I quit work when Mark was born and stayed home until he started first grade. Then, my law degree notwithstanding, I got a job teaching so I could be with my son after school. I scheduled play dates some days, but sometimes I would just keep my son to myself. We'd go to the park or the beach and just enjoy being together. What with graduate school and starting the business, my wife and I got a last start so Mark is our only child. He seemed to like me well enough, so I saw no reason to share him with computer games or those Play Station things. We'd read books or he'd help me in the kitchen. When he started school, I didn't necessarily see him much during the day, but I pretty much knew where he was and who he was with."

"In high school, Mark did well enough, more than well enough really. Three sport athlete, good grades, well-liked by his peers and teachers. I never talked about this with anyone—his mother and I are private people—but there were some quarters when Mark would come home with almost all As. And he was always helping out at the school, organizing fund raisers, getting other kids to join him with all his volunteer activities."

"I'm not claiming credit; I know we got a lucky roll of the dice with this kid: he slept through the night when he was only a few months old; he ate every food we introduced. He never had colic or any health issues as a baby and except for falling off his bike and breaking his collar bone when he was nine and having his appendix out when he was 12, he was never sick a day in his life. He was obviously bright enough. I know there's a genetic component to that too. I just feel lucky and grateful."

"The point is he was just such an easy kid and such a pleasure to be around even into adolescence. Of course, now that he's a senior in high school, he spends more time with his friends than he does with us. That's appropriate and I couldn't be happier. His friends are nice kids, he's chosen well, and they spend their time outdoors playing sports or hiking on the trails outside town. I'm glad he has made good choices and that he's so independent. I don't worry about him; I know he has good judgment. Of course he knows kids who smoke pot every day and play video games for hours on end. But he seems to avoid getting too close with those kids."

"Where I'm stuck is this bit about his going off to college in a few months. Obviously, it's the right thing for him to do. I know he'll do fine in the classroom and out. He's interested in a bunch of subjects; he has good study habits; he makes friends easily. It's not like I'm worried or anything."

"It's just that I'm going to miss him so much."

"I feel like I just got a pink slip. How could I get fired when I didn't do anything wrong?"

***

I don't have anything relevant to add to this loving father's poignant insight into the first 17 years with his son. I think he got it right: it requires moral courage to know that you've done what you could as a parent and that it's time to let go. I also admit that he was lucky. Having a supportive spouse and some economic resources can make all the difference. A single parent working two jobs wouldn't be able to spend as much time with his son.

Hodding Carter said that "there are only two lasting bequests we can hope to give our children. One of these is roots, the other, wings."

I agree with Gretchen Rubin. "The days are long but the years fly." The best time to make a memory with your child is today.

45

"Good Morning;" "Hey, Stupid;" "I Love You"

Any communication can be misinterpreted. Even the simplest of greetings can be processed in multiple ways. "Good morning" can be non-committal, inviting, or threatening. "Good morning" can be heard as an invitation to conversation or as a dismissive end to one. For an example of the contemptuous salutation look no further than an 18th century interaction between strangers of disparate social classes. "Good morning" can unmistakably mean "this conversation is over."

"Hey, Stupid" can be loving or threatening depending on your previous experience—or lack thereof—with the speaker, beloved high school buddy versus imposing stranger at a crowded intersection.

And what about the phrase that should be the most simple and straight forward? Could "I love you" be misinterpreted? Indeed it can. "I love you" can wander all over the place. "I love you" can mean, depending on the context, "Let's spend our lives together," or "Goodbye." "I love you" can even be a bludgeon. "I love you," with the implied, "So why won't you clean the house?" can harm rather than help a couple.

Surely there is a range of ability in understanding what these phrases— "Good morning," "Hey, Stupid," and "I love you"—actually mean. Some folks are better than others at picking up on meaning. Some people are terrible at it. Just like some of my gentle readers are unable to multiply three-digit numbers in their head, some of us have a tough time determining whether "I'll call you right back" actually means "I'll call you right back" or "I don't want to speak to you. Ever."

To make matters worse, add a smidgeon of oppositionality to an adolescent who has had a tough time picking up social skills his whole life. Just like some of you would have a harsher time than others multiplying 123 x 456 without pencil and paper, imagine our 18 year-old slumped on a couch, not making eye contact with a speaker. "I enjoyed my lunch today," she says. And then turns away with a grimace, puts a finger in her mouth, and mimics gagging. If our adolescent doesn't see her pretending to throw up, he isn't going to pick up on her sarcasm. It's a problem.

A problem which can be multiplied ten-fold when our young man with imperfect social skills wants desperately to start dating. "Don't go too fast" he is told by thoughtful adults. "Don't wear your heart on your sleeve." Doubtless, these bromides are good advice for normally achieving 18 year-olds with unimpaired ability to read interpersonal cues.

But what do these phrases actually mean for our young man who doesn't perceive social language the same way you do?

"Everything was going great with that girl" our impaired adolescent opines. "We went to dinner and a movie. I walked her home."

Then he pauses the way you might, gentle reader, if I were waiting for you to tell me what 123 times 456 is. "Now she doesn't want anything to do with me, won't return my texts, and has threatened to contact campus security again if I try to get in touch with her. I don't get it."

"What do you think happened?"

"I haven't any idea, no clue whatsoever. I mean, I love this girl so I told her I love her."

"On your first date?"

"Yes. Of course. I love her so I told her so. When I got home from our date, I called her but she said she was busy and that I should call her later. So I called her ten minutes later, but she still didn't pick up so I kept calling her every ten minutes and sent her texts and emails then, all of a sudden these two guys from campus security were banging on my door saying some garbage about stalking. I mean, what is that about? I just don't get it."

The above scenario might be comical if it weren't so sad. And it's easy to throw a stone at this young man—how could anyone be so oblivious?—until you reflect on just how much trouble you're having doing that multiplication problem in your head.

I can teach you how to multiply three-digit numbers without pencil and paper. I know an algorithm. It'll take us some time, but I'm willing if you are. Good math teachers are persistent and tolerant. We have to be. Similarly, parents of kids with poorly developed social skills have to be patient. Parents have to model perspective taking, process out loud what the other person might be thinking, emphasize empathy. Yelling, "Stop slouching on the couch and make eye contact otherwise you won't know whether or not that woman actually enjoyed her lunch!" is less likely to be effective than gently explaining that a young woman can be put off by hearing "I love you" on the first date.

46

The Harry Harlow School of Parenting

Old School: Take your kids to the market to buy brownie mix. Consider whether the 15-ounce package for two dollars is a better value than the 30-ounce package for $3.59. Politely greet the cashier in the checkout line and introduce your child. Emphasize addressing the employee as "Miss." Demonstrate that all jobs, especially menial ones, have value and are to be respected. Teach child how to measure brownie mix and other ingredients with measuring cups. "If one batch of brownies uses three teaspoons of oil, then how many teaspoons of oil will we need for two batches of brownies?" Seamlessly expose child to how useful and pleasant mathematics can be. Allow child to learn patience waiting for brownies to cool. Play counting games and sing songs to pass the time. Ask child to cut brownies into two inch squares. Inquire whether three rows of four brownies is the same as four rows of three brownies. Consider articulating the phrase "commutative property of multiplication." Send child next door with three hot brownies for elderly neighbors. Allow child to dry and put away mixing bowls and pans after you wash them. Reflect on how great it is that your child is seamlessly acquiring another set of useful skills—cooking, cleaning, and sharing—among them.

The Harry Harlow School of Parenting recommends avoiding this time consuming method that can leave the kitchen a mess. Besides, who has the patience for this shit when "Game of Thrones" is on TV? The Harry Harlow School of Parenting suggests that instead of making brownies with your offspring that you send your nanny to the store to buy ready-made brownies. While the nanny is in the SUV, have your child watch a video of an animated robot making brownies then blowing up the house.

Old School: Take child and family dog to wilderness area on outskirts of town. Throw Frisbee for family dog to retrieve. Lose Frisbee. Teach child colorful language not to be repeated in polite company regarding family dog. Watch dog chase evil squirrels. Wonder aloud whether family dog is actually famous mythological beast, the harpy. Tell mythological story while unpacking lunch from backpack. Turn around because you thought you heard something in the trees over there. Turn back around. Discourage family dog from devouring the remainder of the lunch. Express concern to child about where the other half of the lunch wrapper may have gotten to. Notice one half of lunch wrapper in dog's mouth. Point out to child how the family dog looks both smug and guilty at the same time. Using compass and position of sun, go for long walk with child and family dog. Attempt to teach child orienteering skills. Get hopelessly lost. Tell child story of Odysseus and his return from the Trojan War emphasizing the role of Argos, a family dog who did not, to our knowledge, clandestinely eat all the lunch when out hiking with Telemachus. As sun goes down and weather turns cold, congratulate yourself on having remembered to bring sweaters for both yourself and your child. Reuse colorful language upon reflecting that said sweaters are safely in the backseat of the car. Display and model for child cheerful attitude and good character when thoroughly convinced of how completely and irretrievably lost you are and how dark it is getting. Consider whether the odds of being able to make a fire without matches are one in a hundred or one in a thousand. Discuss elementary probability theory with child. Berate child for interrupting elementary probability theory lecture with the words, "Look, dad. The car is only a hundred yards over there." Teach child about orders of magnitude by counting bug bites.

The Harry Harlow School of Parenting recommends avoiding both bug bites and lost Frisbees by staying home and planting your child in front of the 42" television screen. There are plenty of shows about the outdoors on the nature channel not to mention animations about mythology.

***

A Bit of Background on the Harry Harlow School of Parenting. To study maternal bonding, Harlow separated new-born monkey babies from their mothers, replacing the flesh and blood monkey moms with cloth or wire ones. Unsurprisingly, the monkey babies who grew up without interaction or connection to real-life monkey moms were disturbed; the phrase "monkey psychopaths" comes to mind.

Even half a century later, it is hard to envision a more horrific holocaust of abused animals. Needless to say, the monkeys brought up without contact with other animals, never recovered. They went through their short lives rocking, damaged, and detached. Even when subsequently exposed to other living monkeys, they were unable to interact. They were never anywhere even close to normal.

Stop me if you could have figured this out without torturing generations of primates, but we "attach" to members of our own species—not to inanimate objects made of cloth. This horrific lesson, that human children turn out better if brought up by their actual parents rather than by glowing rectangles, is one that we overlook at our peril.

In short and without irony, it is better to make a mess in the kitchen and be bitten by countless bugs than to let your children be brought up by screens.

There is no substitute for real parenting in real time.

I Read the News Today

Should your adolescent children be encouraged to watch the news on television? Before reminding me that "an informed populace is the hallmark of a strong democracy" think about what you, an adult, get from televised news. Do you acquire information unobtainable elsewhere? Do you learn what is going on in your local community and across the world? Does televised news give you something of value? Does televised news give you a feeling of calm?

Because that's not what I get. When I watch televised news, I just get agitated.

I see injustice, excess, pollution. I see innocents coming to harm and guilty people flourishing. I see adolescents going hungry and children being abused. I see flood, fire, and famine, and doom, despair, and destruction.

I feel one part informed and two parts violated.

Worse, there's nothing I see on the televised news that changes my behavior. Does knowing that there is a shortage of blood products cause you to donate at the blood bank? Televised news isn't convincing me to actually <u>do</u> anything any more than watching Sigourney Weaver in "Aliens" makes me want to go to Neptune to look for minerals.

"If it bleeds, it leads" might be good for ratings but it isn't good for my mental health.

There are other sources—more accurate and calmer sources—from which to learn what's going on in the world. Written news gives me a chance to analyze and reflect. Even more importantly, I can choose what topics I want to focus on. If a headline suggests that a 19 year-old mother has burnt her three-year-old son with a cigarette lighter and then pushed him into a table and killed him, I can skip that story and focus my attention on that which allows me to get through the day. You and I already know of the egregious child abuse going on in our communities. Being pummeled with information doesn't help the child, it just makes the viewer miserable. If I'm watching news on TV, it's too late to turn away.

And it's not just child abuse that is better read about than watched. What about the incessant barrage of information about celebrities? As Mary Pipher points out in a slightly different context, your family may be a pain in the neck, but Jusin Bieber isn't going to come up with a few bucks for you if you're behind on your mortgage. Those professional athletes about whom you know everything, their batting averages, what they studied in college, their salaries? When you've spent three consecutive nights in the hospital with your barfing kid, those same athletes are unlikely to come by and take a shift so that you can get a shower and some rest.

Whether or not you can benefit from the disorienting, disjointed onslaught of painful images on TV, what about your kids? Wouldn't a discussion of events—local and global—be a better way to share your values with your progeny? By bringing up events of the day over the dinner table, you can control the flow of information and the pace of the conversation.

Because you can't take back an image.

Once your children have seen something, there is nothing you can do to allow them to "un-see" it.

By turning off the news, you also communicate to your children that your house is a place where there is time for reflective conversation without uncontrolled invaders. Quite a concept in a world where even restaurants are overrun with blaring screens. The wonderful Spanish expression, "sobre mesa," which means "relaxed conversation after a meal" can't happen if you can't hear one another over the pounding of the TV.

Orwell got it right, as always. In 1984, a book that remains prescient, 66 years after its publication, citizens are required to attend the "two-minute hate" in which they hurl invective at an enemy shown on a huge screen. The "spontaneous overflow of powerful feeling" which Wordsworth never imagined is meant to keep the populace in line with hating an unseen antagonist. The enemy today is the feeling of outrage at that over which we have no control. Or as Bruce Springsteen said, "She didn't get me excited, she just made me feel mean."

Maybe it's time to update Timothy Leary's phrase, "Turn on, tune in, drop out." To bring up healthy families in these perilous times, it might be a better idea to "Turn off, tune out, and drop in"—dropping in on family conversation in particular might be a plus. Leave the disjointed, graphic, and harmful images for those who can't turn off their televisions.

48

Resilience

One of my ultra-marathon buddies said: "I've always believed that I can win any race if the event is long enough. I'm never going to be the fastest and I'm never going to be the strongest, but I believe I can keep putting one foot in front of the other longer than anyone else."

Where does resilience of this depth come from?

This example is from a well-known novella. For those of you who were not ninth graders in my English class when I started teaching in 1978, here is a synopsis of <u>The Old Man and the Sea</u>: Santiago, an elderly and desperately poor fisherman, has not caught a fish in three months. Hungry and alone he sails hours and hours off the coast of his small village in Cuba, believing that his luck will change with increased risk. Indeed after hours alone drifting in the gulf stream, he hooks the fish of a lifetime—an enormous, magnificent marlin. If he can land this fish, he will not only have enough money for food, but he will also be known as the bravest and toughest—true encomiums in Hemingway's masculine world.

An epic encounter ensues, man against nature. Santiago battles the marlin, holding on to ropes until his hands bleed. Hours turn into days as the glorious animal fights for his life. Fatigued, at the end of his strength, and dehydrated to the point of delirium, Santiago triumphs. The fish is his. Santiago lashes the fish to the side of his small skiff and begins the journey back to the island.

Which is where the real trouble begins.

Because in the night, his prize marlin is attached by sharks.

With only a knife attached to an oar, Santiago kills shark after ravenous shark. When the knife breaks, Santiago protects his fish by beating sharks to death with the damaged oar. Even when the oar is lost, Santiago continues to fight the sharks.

But the sharks are too many and too relentless. In the fullness of time, the sharks have eaten every ounce of flesh from what was once the most extraordinary fish ever caught in the Caribbean. Santiago returns to his village half dead from hunger and fatigue. Carrying the mast of his boat up the beach to his shack, he has to stop five times. Bloodied but unbroken, he sleeps.

From the last page of the novel:

That afternoon there was a party of tourists at the Terrace and looking down in the water among the empty beer cans and dead barracudas a woman saw a great long white spine with a huge tail at the end that lifted and swung with the tide while the east wind blew a heavy steady sea outside the entrance to the harbour.

"What's that?" she asked a waiter and pointed to the long backbone of the great fish that was now just garbage waiting to go out with the tide.

"Tiburon," the waiter said. "Shark." He was meaning to explain what had happened.

"I didn't know sharks had such handsome, beautifully formed tails."

"I didn't either," her male companion said.

***

In other words, they don't get it.

The tourists don't understand. They don't understand the nature of Santiago's epic struggle; they don't understand the dignity of hard work; they don't understand that even in abject defeat, Santiago is not defined by his hunger nor by his poverty. They don't understand that his triumph is magnificent and real, even if no one witnessed it or knows about it.

Which brings me—"finally" you could well say—to my thoughts about parenting for this essay: it's okay if no one understands how you're raising your kids. It's okay if nobody else gets it.

If you're trying to raise resilient kids, you may have to go against the popular culture that encourages you to buy meaningless baubles for your children. If you're trying to raise kids who don't give up, you may have to go strike out against your neighbors who succumb to their children's every whine.

If all the other parents say "okay" to an invitation to take second graders to a birthday party at Dandy Bear in a limousine, you can say, "no, thank you." If all the other parents are watching reality shows with their kids, you can say, "We don't watch that." And if all the other parents allow their children to play video games, you can stand up and say, "In our home, we have a no-screen policy."

There may be rumbles and grumbles at first. There may even be that kid down the block who doesn't want to come over to your house if he can't play video games. (It might be argued that this loss would not be insurmountable.)

You don't need anyone else's understanding or permission regarding how to bring up your kids. And doesn't that sound like the first step in raising resilient children who can stand up for themselves?

49

It's the Relationship, Stupid

An attractive 30-something bank employee approached me as I stood in line at the teller window yesterday. "Interest rates have never been lower," she began without preamble. As our previous interactions had never exceeded conversations of the "Nice day" variety, I was intrigued by her wide-eyed enthusiasm. "There has never been a better time to make the equity in your home work for you!" she continued with an urgency usually reserved for informing sleeping occupants about their burning home.

With only the vaguest hope of being able to retire before my 90th birthday, I need more debt like I need more worn out running shoes. Still, it would have been rude to interrupt.

"Let's do it now!" she concluded fervently. Not certain if she wanted to sell me a home equity line or have sex with me on the brightly lit tile floor of the savings and loan, I gently suggested that I was not interested. I did not point out that "NINJA" (no income, no job) loans were part of an execrable system of impropriety and excess that nearly brought our country to its financial knees. Loaning egregious sums of money to people who had no hope of repaying was a bad plan five years ago and remains malicious today. "Thank you for thinking of me" I said with all the restraint I could muster.

I don't fault the exuberant assistant manager. Obviously, she was just reciting lines forced on her from her corporate office. I envisioned her training at an endless Saturday seminar: "Then, look the customer directly in the eye and say, 'Let's do it now!'" She has to make a living; lower level bank employees probably don't earn a bunch. The bank has to make money too. My interest for a column on parenting has to do with the fact that, were I to purchase a loan, the interests of the 30-something employee would be served; mine would not.

When you tell your child to do something, who benefits? Before you say, "I only want what's best for my children," think deeply and critically. If your child does what you suggest, does he profit? Or do you?

Of course, there's plenty of overlap between what's good for your kids and what's good for you. I can proclaim that I want my adolescent children to help clear the table and wash the dishes because I'm teaching them valuable skills that will be necessary when they live on their own. But the fact of the matter is I just want some help with the endless stream of pots and pans. I can say that I want my toddler to get to bed by eight o'clock so that she will be on a schedule and be able to regulate her sleep cycle, but what I really want is for her to go to bed so that I can have some time to myself to read a book or return a call.

The situation gets murkier on the athletic field and in the classroom. Why do you want so desperately for your daughter's U-12 soccer team to beat those other kids (many of whom you've known since birth?) It's developmentally appropriate to learn to lose graciously. It's damaging to kids to hear their parents raging "Kill the ref!"

In the world of kids playing formal sports, it is hard to exaggerate the egregious, psychotic screaming that passes for supportive parenting. My favorite offensive comment from the mother of a girl on a winning team was, "They needed that." No they didn't, mom. They're little girls and they're fond of the other little girls in the uniforms of the other color. <u>You</u> are the one who needed that.

And frankly, it makes me wonder if you shouldn't find another hobby that doesn't involve hoping that a group of nine-year-olds doesn't win a soccer game.

My second favorite remark was from the mother of a lovely young client of mine whose big heart and graciousness were exceeded only by his inability to decipher and understand the written word. Seth and I had worked hard to come up with a list of colleges with learning support where he could thrive. When Seth presented the schools to his mother, she said, "He can't go to those schools; no one at my country club has ever heard of any of them."

Even a stray dog knows if it has been tripped over or kicked. Don't you think your children know if you want them to get good grades because you want what's best for them or because you want to show off their accomplishments to your friends?

And if you are, in Alfie Kohn's wonderful phrase, "basking in reflected glory," don't you think your children perceive the disconnect? Don't you think they know that they are loved for what they do rather than who they are?

Just like I recognized the attractive woman at the bank for who she was— someone trying to sell me a second mortgage I didn't need with a memorized pitch and a fake smile.

50

Pay Me Now or Pay Me Later

The son of a farmer has done a service—saving the kingdom from invaders, perhaps, or slaying a particularly recalcitrant dragon—and the king is grateful. The king insists that, as repayment for his heroic deed, the farmer's son accept a gift, any gift he desires. Gold, jewels, land, wealth beyond imagining and of any description, will be bestowed upon the farmer's son just for the asking. All the farmer's son has to do is name that which he desires. Clever lad that he is—after all, he was able to rescue the imperiled kingdom—the farmer's son insists on being given only a grain of rice.

"One grain of rice is not enough!" the king exclaims. "I insist that your reward be commensurate with the extraordinary service you have performed. Name something of more value."

"As you wish, Highness," the farmer's son replies. "I just happen to have here a chessboard." The farmer's son produces a standard chessboard from under his tunic. "I ask only for one grain of rice to be placed on the first square of the chess board. I ask for twice as many grains of rice as on each subsequent square."

"Could you say that again slowly?" the king asks politely.

"My pleasure, Eminence," the farmer's son replies. "One grain of rice on the first square, two grains of rice on the second square, four grains of rice on the third square, and so on. Each square on the chess board will have twice as many grains as the square before."

The farmer's son produces a stylus (apparently tunics were more commodious in those days) and scratches the following numbers in the sand.

1, 2, 4...

"It shall be done," cries the king. Who comes to regret his hasty largesse when he understands the following simple arithmetic: An eight by eight chessboard has 64 squares. One grain of rice on the first square, two grains of rice on the second square, and four grains of rice on the third square leads inexorably to $9.2233720368548 \times 10^{18}$ or approximately 9,223,372,036,854,800,000 grains of rice on the 64th square. How much rice is 9,223,372,036,854,800,000 grains? 9,223,372,036,854,800,000 grains is more rice than ever has been or ever will be grown on the planet Earth. 9,223,372,036,854,800,000 grains of rice is more grains than there are stars in our galaxy. Lots more.

In short, a whole bunch of rice.

Bear with me gentle reader while I switch narrative gears and share the story of a lovely, imaginative, clever lad filled with his mother's analytical insight (she's an engineer) and his father's creative intuition (he works at an art gallery.) Alex is loved by his parents both of whom work outside the home. From an early age, Alex's parents have exposed him to interactive screens. Alex is a sophisticated Minecraft affectionado; he sends texts and emails to his similarly well behaved friends; he uses the Internet to look up stuff for school projects and to view videos on YouTube.

Concerned that Alex is relying too much on screens and not enough on interacting with other actual humans, his parents introduce a zero tolerance policy for screens on Alex's tenth birthday. Easy going, good kid that he is, Alex misses his email and texts and his interactive games. He asks his parents repeatedly why he can no longer play Minecraft or other video games. He incessantly asks his parents why he can't have his devices. He is unbearable to live with, constantly asking for access to his games and electronic communication. He is disappointed and fussy.

For one whole day.

His parents, who have replaced the screens with swimming lessons, a church group, reading <u>Harry Potter and the Sorcerer's Stone</u> out loud, building a fire pit in the backyard, and a series of weekend hikes with the family, notice that within 24-hours, Alex doesn't miss his screens in the least.

Just down the road from Alex lives Brandon. Brandon's parents were in the same Lamaze class as Alex's parents although Brandon was born one month to the day before his neighbor. Brandon was also playing murder simulator video games although he was not yet involved in the one in which the player gets extra points if, after having sex with a prostitute, he beats her up rather than pays her. Brandon's parents also made their home a "screen free zone" replacing "World of Warcrack" with a cooking class, the Percy Jackson book series, yard work, a chemistry set, and a soccer league. When the change was instituted, Brandon was thoroughly upset. He whined and negotiated. He had a complete temper tantrum.

For two solid, unbearable days.

And then he was fine with his new interactive activities.

***

Perhaps the more insightful of my gentle readers will discern where this narrative is going.

Caleb is ten years and two months old. It will take him four days to get over the new "no screens" policy in his home. Darren in ten years and three months old. It may take him four days to "detox" from his reliance on screens.

1, 2, 4...

At some point, it becomes impossible to wean your kid from their reliance on murder simulators and the addictive stimulation of screens. For ten-year-olds, it takes a day or so to overcome screen dependence. For 17 year-olds it might take 9,223,372,036,854,800,000 days. Seventeen year-olds are generally less compliant and less reliant on the good opinion of their parents. By 17 years of age, children can typically drive cars, make their own arrangements, and use computers outside the home. They are also a lot snarkier and strong-willed than they were at age 10. In short, it may be impossible to keep a 17-year-old away from playing "Halo" every day after school and all day on the weekends.

And don't even try to tell me about playing "Grand Theft Auto" for just a few minutes each day. Ask anyone who has ever tried to use "just a little" cocaine if this is a viable plan.

You know the old expression, "pay me now or pay me later"?

Now is cheaper.

51

Eyes on the Prize

In 1962, James Meredith became the first Black man to attend the University of Mississippi. Just prior to Mr. Meredith's enrollment, the Governor of Mississippi, Ross Barnett, tried to convince the president of the United States that Meredith should not be allowed to matriculate. The governor, representing the opinion of many folks in his state, felt strongly that black students and white students should not drink from the same water fountains let alone attend class together.

A transcript of their phone call survives. President Kennedy is unflaggingly polite, but he does not waver in his conviction that Meredith be allowed to start school.

In addition to its historical significance—Thurgood Marshall, Andrew Young and Barack O'Bama didn't happen by themselves—this conversation is notable for what is not said. President Kennedy does not say to Governor

Barnett: "I am the president of the United States of America; I have the legal and the moral authority to make you do what I say."

Nor does Kennedy say, "You backwoods, inbred, one-eyed, racist, thudpucker, I will crush you like the insignificant vermin that you are. Your family will suffer for generations untold for fighting me on this issue."

Kennedy certainly doesn't say, "I thought we were friends, you hurt my feelings, why can't you see this my way?"

The president sticks to the point—Black students will start at the University of Mississippi. In today's terms he is "on message." The president doesn't debate, he doesn't use his listening skills, he doesn't seem overly concerned about whether or not Governor Barnett is going to send his family a card next Christmas. Because in a very real sense, there is nothing to talk about. The marines and the National Guard—thousands of men with loaded rifles—are not referenced explicitly, but both men in the conversation know the location of those men and their rifles. The president has made a decision. Whether or not Governor Barnett is pleased about the decision is less important to the president.

***

There are many instances when you can—and should—evoke consensus with your children, listen to dissenting opinions, and allow children to have their voices heard so that they can develop self-advocacy skills. "Would you like another piece of chicken?" (Okay, let's be more realistic: "Would you like another brownie?") "Would you like to wear the blue shirt of the red shirt?" (Note that attending first grade naked is not an option.) "Would you like to invite Sophia and her family to your quince?" "Would you like to take a calculus course?" Of course parents must understand that sometimes adolescents make imperfect choices and that both generation must be prepared to live with the consequences.

Other times parents must be on message with your kids. There are a small number of topics on which debate is contra-indicated. Matters of health is an example. Especially when your kids bring home garbage like the following.

"Mom, all the other kids are smoking pot. Adults drink, kids should be able to smoke pot. Marijuana is in the Bible. And it's legal in Colorado. And I know lots of kids who smoke pot and do good in school. Marijuana is good

178

for you; glaucoma and cancer patients need it. Lots of famous people smoke marijuana and they're happy. There's nothing wrong with marijuana. All your friends smoked marijuana in college and none of them are like brain damaged or anything. Both teams in the super bowl this year were from the only two states to have legalized pot. Why can't I just try pot and if I don't like it I won't do it anymore? You're so mean. I'm not going to have any friends. Everybody else smokes pot…"

And on and on.

Now would be a good time not to address any of these arguments—some of which are dumber than others, all of which are completely vacuous. The message is simple and straight forward. Just as Kennedy doesn't allude to the marines and the loaded rifles, parents don't need to articulate that they will not support their child economically or emotionally should she choose to smoke pot.

No one is arguing against medicinal marijuana. No one is suggesting that the war on drugs is winnable. No one is disagreeing that marijuana is any better or worse than alcohol. No one is discounting that there are some functioning adults who smoke pot. No one is insisting that every marijuana user goes on to harder drugs. Your position, as loving parents, is only that in your family, teenagers don't get to choose to smoke pot. I believe the expression is "Not on my watch."

Having articulated your position twice a year or so, there is nothing left to talk about: James Meredith IS going to attend class at the University of Mississippi. Your kids are NOT going to smoke pot. If they choose to use, they can do so somewhere else with someone else's support.

It's time to be on the right side of history on this one. Half a century after James Meredith walked up the steps to the University of Mississippi, no reasonable person would agree with Governor Barnett that college classes should be separated by race. History will tell us that insisting your kids stay away from pot was also the right call.

52

The Sound of Silence

What is the one sound that resonates more than any other? What is the one sound that no one can ignore? What is the one sound that makes everyone respond viscerally, at the deepest level below conscious awareness?

A jet engine is annoying, loud, disturbing, unpleasant. Firecrackers going off can disturb your sleep and make you want to speak to those annoying neighbors about their feral children. Listening to a poorly trained violinist can make you rethink your belief in a just and merciful deity. Your Aunt Minnie's unrelenting litany of complaints about her health has caused many a man to want to put a fork through his ear.

But there is another sound that is more cogent than any of these.

When US troops attacked a compound harboring foreign bad guys, they played loud rock music. Just learning the play list, I was ready to surrender.

But there's another sound that would have been even more likely to cause the enemy combatants to throw down their rifles.

Give up?

The one sound that causes all of us to respond more quickly, more viscerally, and more emphatically than any other is that of a baby crying.

Even if the baby is not yours. Even if you don't have children of your own. Even if you're a 19-year-old fraternity pledge who couldn't distinguish a baby from an empty pizza box. Even if you don't particularly like babies.

The sound of a baby crying is more cogent, more compelling, more profound than fire crackers, jet engines, trucks backfiring, or your cousin Minnie with the digestive issues.

It's not hard to understand why. In our evolutionary adaptive environment, there was an advantage to responding to the very real needs of our progeny. Those who ignored their kids were less likely to have their genes passed on to their grandchildren.

Which is not to say that while taking the trash buckets out to the curb having only told their able bodied 16-year-old son to be responsible on Monday and Thursday morning about a million times that even the most loving parent hasn't wished that her child were devoured by a saber tooth tiger.

The tricky bit for loving parents is knowing when to set the limit, to understand that "no" is a complete sentence. Ignoring well-meaning friends who mistake permissiveness for affection is critical as well.

"How can you deny your child cake at her second birthday party?" they will ask. Rather than explain that in your home, you prefer fruit to icing, just go ahead, stand up, and do what's right for your child. (Although I sometimes wonder if these same people just enjoy saying "you're raising your kids wrong" no matter what you do and—were you to serve cake instead of fruit—would object just the same.) How can you deny your 12-year-old child unlimited access to "Shoot, Shoot, Shoot, Blood, Blood, Blood, Kill, Kill,Kill?"

Easy. Watch me.

A baby's every need should be dealt with immediately. A tired baby needs to sleep, a hungry baby needs to be fed, a wet baby needs to be changed, and a fussy baby needs to be hugged and soothed. A 12-year-old's <u>needs</u> (food, clothing, shelter, affection, and camping trips with grumbling parents) must be distinguished from his <u>wants</u> (three hours a day of "Shoot, Shoot, Shoot, Blood, Blood, Blood, Kill, Kill,Kill.")

Feeling that hard wired, age old empathy and addressing your baby's every need is a good thing. Giving in to that which is damaging and dangerous for your adolescent children just so they'll stop fussing may lead to increasing demands that can never be assuaged.

53

Rejection

The University of Pennsylvania accepted 3551 students this year out of 35,788 applicants. The ratio, of about 9.9%, is simple to explain arithmetically—one kid in ten got admitted—harder to process emotionally if you are one of the nine who was not. If your family member got the "we're sorry; there were so many qualified applicants this year" letter, it's hard to acknowledge the simple, blinding truth: U Penn gets a lot of qualified applicants. They don't have room for all of them. Valedictorians were denied; students with 1600 on their SAT were denied; yearbook editors were denied; captains of football teams were denied.

Valedictorians with 1600 SATs who were captain of the football team and editor of the yearbook were denied.

What is the best way to beat these daunting odds? Here's how to make getting into a top college as painless as possible. (The following may not be the answer you wanted, but after 30 years of counseling, I can assure you that it's truer than true.)

1) Don't tell anyone under any circumstances where you're applying. Not ever. No matter what.

You'd be better off publicizing your bracket predictions or the fact that you anticipate spending time with Sofia Vergara in a hot tub. Admittedly, the odds of your being right about who wins every game in the basketball tournament (approximately 1 in 9.22×10^{19}) are easier to calculate than whether or not the star of "Modern Family" will join you in the Jacuzzi, but either way you're setting yourself up to look like an idiot. Whether or not you win the admissions lottery is the same premise. Keep your mouth shut. None of your snarky, competitive classmates can make fun of you if the list of schools to which you've applied is a family secret.

The entrance ways to the bedroom and bathroom in your home have doors. There's a reason for that. It's the same reason that well brought up high school seniors don't discuss their list of schools with anyone with whom they don't share DNA.

"You know that kid, the one who took five APs as a junior, got a 1600 on her SAT and was captain of the lacrosse team? Did you hear that she applied to Dartmouth and got rejected?"

No one can talk about where you got rejected if they don't know where you applied.

And don't even tell me that you "only told your best friend and made her promise not to tell anyone else." You might as well publish a front page ad in the paper.

Here's some extra-credit advice: if you do get a particularly lucky roll of the dice and get admitted to Harvard (5.9% this year) and Columbia (6.9%) keep your mouth shut anyway. Nobody likes a braggart. Classy kids put themselves in the shoes of the less lucky and accept good news graciously. And quietly.

2) Don't ask why.

It makes more sense to ask why, when your thimble was on Short Line Railroad, you ended up on Boardwalk after a roll of four rather than rolling a seven, passing "Go", collecting $200 and picking a card from "Community Chest." You got rejected from U Penn. So did nine out of ten other highly qualified, hardworking, smart young people. Accept that there is a highly arbitrary, random aspect to admissions decisions. Yes, Tommy, the valedictorian and captain of the football team from North Cornstalk High with a 1600 on the SAT was admitted to U Penn. But Timmy, the valedictorian and captain of the football team from South Cornstalk High with a 1600 on the SAT was not. You don't know why Tommy got in and Timmy didn't? Neither do I. Neither does anyone who works in admissions at the University of Pennsylvania.

3) Who you are is more important than where you go.

The saddest scam ever was when the parents of severely autistic, non-communicative children were told that the kids could actually converse if were hooked up to a Ouija Board and "helped" to express themselves by a trained practitioner. Of course, nothing of the kind is possible. A child who can neither read nor speak cannot express himself with a Ouija Board. I have played board games with developmentally delayed children whose mothers-despite repeated entreaties to let the kid alone—were unable to stop "helping" their kids strategize or move pieces.

Being admitted to a "name" school is as important to a top kid as a cognitively impaired child beating a 58-year-old educational consultant at a board game. A strong student will still do well by every meaningful measure wherever she goes to college. Just as the developmentally delayed child will continue to have issues to overcome even if he "wins" one game thanks to his well-intentioned mom. The kids with ability and motivation do well.

Even if they don't get admitted to U. Penn.

54

Driven Kids

Every day during Spring Break, Victor painted lines on the athletic field and changed air conditioner filters at his school. Then he painted a potting shed and two dugouts before moving on to paint a fence around the perimeter of the institution. Although Victor—at age 16—was not a member of the United States Navy, he did come to feel that during his work day, "If something moves, salute it. If it doesn't move, paint it."

As a result of his efforts, Victor was rewarded with more money than any teenager had ever earned in the history of Western Civilization, more money than Napoleon had when he owned some of the nicer bits of Europe. After nine days of painting and more painting, Victor received a check for $450. An equivalent amount for you or me gentle reader would be approximately $450 million. Maybe more. Victor had enough money for five tanks of gas, three movie dates, and a new volleyball. In short, Victor had infinite money, enough to last for months to come. When was the last time you, as an adult, ever had so much money that you could buy anything and everything you wanted into the future?

Victor had recently purchased a "brand new" 2007 Corolla with only 71,000 miles on it. His parents had chipped in a significant percentage for the seven-year-old Toyota, but Victor had "skin in the game." The family—after some discussion—had agreed that Victor would be responsible for 10 percent of the purchase price, 50 percent of maintenance costs, and 100 percent of gas, insurance, and repairs. On the way home from the last day of work in his "new" car, the check for the greatest amount of money ever in the history of the world tucked safely beside him in the front seat, disaster struck: Stopped at a traffic signal, Victor accelerated into the car in front of him. He was only going four miles an hour, but he damaged the front bumper of his car.

The cost of the repair was $430, almost the entirety of Victor's life savings. Victor's attitude was philosophical. "At least I have twenty dollars" he said.

"No you don't," replied his father. "I took your car in to the body shop because you were in school." Victor looked concerned waiting for the other shoe to implode. "You have to take me for ice cream."

Considering the economics of his father's appetite for all things frozen, Victor was again insightful: "Now I know what it's like to be an American," he said. "Always in debt."

Subsequent to the incident at the stop light, Victor has done some work for neighbors: walking dogs, removing tree stumps, mowing lawns. He still swears he will never paint anything again, whether it moves or not. Victor is able to budget his affairs pretty well. When he runs low on cash he stops going to movies with his friends and finds more work. His father likes to believe that Victor may live a long, happy life without ever viewing "Crash, Boom, Bang" or whatever helicopter abusive film is in the theaters lately and sees no reason to supplement Victor's earnings.

At the risk of overstating the obvious, compare Victor's narrative with that of "Carl," an ungrateful, snarky child to begin with who, making no contribution whatsoever, was given a 2014 V6, 3.7 L Mustang convertible (manufacturer's suggested retail price, $41,975) by his generous, but clueless parents. Although Carl is only 15 and therefore, cannot legally drive, his parents helped him overlook this annoying technicality and facilitated his procuring a counterfeit driver's license. Carl promptly destroyed the 2014 Mustang

187

convertible by driving into a telephone pole—Hey, it wasn't his fault; he honked!—only to receive another 2014 V6, 3.7 L Mustang convertible the next weekend.

I certainly hope Carl will be responsible with this second Mustang and not drive while impaired. That Carl's parents impress me as permanently impaired because who, in their right mind, gives a car like that to an underage driver, is perhaps the subject of another essay. In any case, if Carl does go drag racing and kill a few people, it won't be his fault because cars don't kill people; people do.

I will argue that Victor is more likely to have a reasonable life than is Carl. Yes, I agree that "reasonable life" is a silly expression and no, I can't pretend to know what the phrase means exactly. But I bet you could make a good guess. Victor will have a reasonable life knowing the price of many things and the value of some others. Carl will not. Carl will never be satisfied no matter what he is given. Not for more than a few minutes anyway.

There is lots of talk these days about consequences and responsibility. I would argue that Victor knows more about consequences than Carl does. "If you hit someone with your car even at four miles per hour, you will lose all your money" is what Victor understands. "If you smack your car into a telephone pole, you get another car" is what Carl knows.

That Carl's parents TALK to him about responsibility, I have no doubt. But I would argue that HEARING about consequences is like hearing about sex. I am told that actually having sex is both more instructive and more interesting than hearing about it.

Directed advice: next time your son tries to pull at your heart strings and tells you that "all the other kids" have $41,975 Mustangs, tell him to go pick up a paint brush. Later, you might even get some ice cream.

55

Refer Madness

When a poor child is abused, the neighbors hear about it; the walls are thin, the community small. When a wealthy child is abused, the neighbors don't know because their houses are too far apart.

There are those who suggest that there is a qualitative difference between the kind of abuse that goes on—deprivation in one neighborhood, neglect in another. I am less sure.

It has often been remarked that when poor people use a form of cocaine called crack, they go to jail but that when wealthy people use cocaine they go to community service.

Today's conversation involves what drug addiction—which is linked to child abuse in many ways—looks like across income classes. See if you can perceive any similarities between the narratives of those of disparate social status. I can discern a difference between where the stories start out—large house in the suburbs versus small apartment in the inner city—but there appears to be no difference in where the victims end up.

When a poor kid gets into drugs, it's easy to point a finger, find fault. "He had no role models;" "the drugs were readily available;" "drug education is lacking." These "reasons" may be as sketchy as they are incomplete.

Contrast your inferences about children about whom you have no direct experience with the following narrative that I have heard repeatedly for the past 30 years: "My child just smokes a little pot. What's wrong with that? Everyone smokes pot. Everyone knows marijuana is not addictive. Everyone knows marijuana is not a gateway drug. Sure, some people go on to harder drugs after starting with marijuana, but most don't. Those people who steal to get high are from bad neighborhoods. Those people should go to jail. But we're different. Sure, my daughter took money from my wallet and jewelry from her grandmother but we did not prosecute. My daughter can't go to jail. What kind of people do you think we are? We couldn't let our daughter get lost in the legal system. So then when my daughter stole an iPad from a classmate, we hired a great criminal defense attorney. My child did not spend one minute in jail. Now we're working to have the record expunged."

With the passage of time and without intervention, the story of this unfortunate family continues. "I can't imagine how my daughter ended up living with that mid-level drug dealer. She's pregnant. Again. It's likely that this baby will be developmentally delayed as well. The other child is 18 months old now, but he hasn't spoken a word and he shows no sign of walking. The pediatrician said that the alcohol, marijuana, and oxycontin that my daughter took when she was pregnant may have something to do with our grandchild's difficulties. And our daughter is unable or unwilling to stop using prescription painkillers with this pregnancy either."

"If the boyfriend is arrested again—he makes his living stealing prescription drugs and selling them—how will she support the babies? How did we get to this horrible place? When our daughter was in high school, whenever we smoked marijuana with her, we told her to only do it in moderation like we do."

At the risk of overstating the obvious, here is where these parents went horribly wrong. "Do as I say, not as I do" never works. If you use, chances are your kids will too. Don't even try to tell me that your kids don't know about your stash of marijuana or the painkillers you've been using. By the time your kids hit middle school, they know. They know exactly what you're doing in the garage when you think they're asleep.

What should these parents have done differently? For starters, they should have stood up earlier. They should have allowed their daughter to deal with the consequences of her incipient addiction early on, before her substance abuse took on a life of its own and morphed into full blown chemical dependency. "The best way to stop is not to start." It's hard for these parents to withdraw support now; the pattern of enabling is too ingrained. When the boyfriend goes to jail, how will their daughter and the grandchild survive? It would have been easier to communicate the lessons earlier on; now it may be too late.

Many of my gentle readers have pointed out that my anti-drug screeds lack universal validity. "Medical marijuana is helpful for cancer patients" they point out. "Would YOU want your loved ones who had an operation not to have access to morphine when in recovery?" "Lots of people smoke marijuana and lead productive lives." "Who are you to tell people what they can and can not do?"

Each of these arguments may hold some truth. That truth will be of small comfort to the family described above. Drugs are an "equal opportunity destroyer." When living in poverty with a developmentally delayed child and another on the way, it no longer matters whether or not some people smoke pot occasionally and productively. Just as it doesn't matter whether or not the mom described above grew up in a big house or a small apartment.

56

Love the One You're With

Can you even imagine anything worse than your annoying job? You know the one I mean. That job you go to every single, stupid day with the insensitive boss and the inept subordinates. The job that requires you to bring work home to finish at night and on the weekends, the job that made you miss your daughter's soccer game when her team made the playoffs. The job that pays you less than you were making five years ago, the job with the lousy benefits and insulting retirement plan.

The only thing worse than your unbearable job would be not having a job.

Can you imagine anything worse than waking up at oh dark hundred to go sweating through a fetid swamp with a swarmy pack of middle aged, paunchy, balding men? Running with a group of guys who think "Don't tell those religious zealots any 'knock, knock' jokes" is the funniest thing since the Marx Brothers? Tromping through the humidity, dodging bat-sized mosquitoes, grunting with each aching step. What could be worse than trying to stave off inevitable mortality one tedious step after another?

The only thing worse than lacing up those sneakers in the dark would be the higher risk for heart disease resulting from not plodding through the bog those early mornings. Sleeping in and inhaling doughnuts would be, in the long term, worse.

Here's the most important one: the only thing worse than your sober life—a life filled with doubt and angst, a life replete with unresolved anxieties and concerns about the future, concerns about the children—would be a life of addiction.

Sneaking drinks, blacking out, losing days of your life to blurry memories of shameful behavior. Acquiring risk of kidney failure or sudden, violent death. That was worse.

"Life is much to be endured, little to be enjoyed" said Dr. Johnson.

The movies teach us that "if only" then everything would be ideal. If only Susie would go out with me. If only Susie would fall in love with me. If only Susie would marry me. If only Susie would do things the way I say. If only Susie weren't so completely unreasonable and impossible to live with. If only Susie would divorce me. If only Susie would accept this perfectly reasonable dissolution of assets agreement. If only Susie would stop suing me for child support.

As the therapists say, "No matter where you go, there you are."

"Sideways" is a pleasant enough film, but the idea that the alcoholic protagonist will live happily ever after thanks to the love of a good woman is naïve. The would-be author learns that his book has been rejected for publication so he guzzles from a bucket of spat out wine. His life will not be better as a result of his book being published. His life would be better if he got over his issue with alcohol which is exacerbated by stress. His book was rejected so he drank. If his book had been accepted, he would have gotten drunk to celebrate. He would have gotten drunk if the moon was in Aquarius. Or not.

Our issues will not leave us from external sources because our issues are not themselves external.

But what if I had a million dollars? With a million dollars I could resolve my debt once and for all; I could make charitable contributions. I wouldn't have to worry about where that sixty thousand dollars is going to come from for that tuition payment this year. Wouldn't I be happier if I won the lottery?

Maybe. Briefly. But I'd still be who I am.

Eighty-five percent of people who receive big payouts—from personal injury settlements, from inheritance, from lottery wins—are right back where they started within 18 months. Every last dollar is gone.

So if having a better job, marrying the girl of your dreams, staying healthy, staying sober aren't what ultimately make a difference, what hope is there for having a good relationship with your children? Again, the only thing worse than your current relationship with your kids would be some other relationship with your kids. Those people down the street who seem content? Don't count on it We never saw what Ward and June Cleaver did when the doors were closed and the cameras turned off. Maybe it's just as well.

If you can't model contentment for your kids, at least avoid suggesting that "everything would be better if only." You would get along with your daughter better if she would clean her room? You would be more accepting of your son if he would do his homework? These are bad plans. Loving your kids for who they are rather than what they do is healthier for everyone involved.

Which is not to suggest that loving parents accept anything less than the best effort from their children. But exertion is a more meaningful measure than result.

"A man's reach should exceed his grasp." But there's no point in being a damn fool about it because your arms don't extend to heaven.

I'm not arguing that you be content with mediocrity. Only that you accept that you, and the people you love, are very likely doing the best that they possibly can. And that surface change would be—almost by definition—only skin deep.

57

Hark, I Hear the Canons Roar!

After years of kicking around auditions and struggling to survive waiting tables, Oscar gets his big break. It's a small part admittedly—actually only one line—but for the first time, he has the chance to act in a real show. On Broadway, no less.

Oscar attends every rehearsal and practices his line like no one has ever practiced before. "Hark, I hear the cannons roar!" he says over and over again in front of the mirror in his tiny fifth floor walk-up. He works endlessly with the director, changing the emphasis on the words of his debut. "HARK! I hear the cannons roar!" "Hark! I HEAR the cannons roar!" "Hark! I hear the cannons ROAR!"

Envisioning being noticed by one of the many critics in the audience on opening night, Oscar is nervous but ready. No aspiring actor has ever practiced harder; no performer has ever been better prepared.

The curtain opens; Oscar walks confidently to the middle of the stage; he turns to face the packed house; BOOM! The cannons go off. Startled out of his wits, Oscar jumps a foot in the air and screams. "What the hell was that!"

***

Oscar wasn't ready. All his preparation, all his hard work, all his willingness came to naught. We wanted to do well; he wanted to get it right, but he didn't. Indeed, he failed miserably. I just don't know how long it will be before he gets another chance at a part in a Broadway show. Indeed, based on his performance with "Hark! I hear the cannons roar!" he may never get another chance.

***

Racso has been making tremendous progress in treatment. He truly feels he had finally kicked his addiction to marijuana. After smoking pot several times a day for years, Racso has now been clean for six full months. Racso religiously attends narcotics anonymous meetings; Racso never misses an appointment with his therapist; Racso even wants to go back to college to be certified as a trained addictions counselor after he has been clean for another year or so. Racso knows how to stay sober when he is elated; Racso knows how to stay sober when he is bored; Racso knows how to stay sober through a host of emotions and situations.

One night after a 12-step meeting, Racso walks outside with a cute girl whom he has seen on previous Monday nights. They get to talking about recovery and go for coffee. The girl invites Racso up to her apartment. They are sitting together on her couch when she offers him marijuana.

BOOM!

Racso wakes up 36 hours later, his life in shambles. He took one puff of marijuana, then another, then a bunch more. He and the cute girl from the meeting made love, smoked some more pot, inhaled a pizza, had sex again, then smoked some more pot. Stoned out of his mind, Racso has slept through his job, gotten fired, and failed to fulfill a number of other commitments that had taken months to put together. Without a paycheck, he is going to have a tough time paying his rent and experience real time consequences.

How could he have known that the cute girl was using and would ask her to join him in getting schnockered? "I like to meet guys at meetings," she said. "They're always so nice, not rude like the guys I meet in bars."

Poor Racso. I hope he gets another chance as sobriety just as I hope that Oscar gets another shot at a part in a Broadway play.

Addicts in recovery have to expect the unexpected. They have to be prepared for "triggers"—people or situations that will set them back. Racso was okay with his job, his budget, his meetings, and his life. He never suspected that a cute girl and the opportunity to smooch would set him spiraling down a familiar path. Now Racso is holed up in his apartment, smoking pot for breakfast, lunch and dinner, eating chocolate ice cream, promising himself that he'll get up early and look for a new job "tomorrow". His self-esteem is lower than a snake's belly in a wagon rut. He feels bad about himself, so he smokes some more pot. His depression keeps him from getting out of bed before the crack of noon. I'm not sure what's going to happen when the rent comes due on the first.

The take away for loving parents is simple: teach your kids that the best way to stop is not to start. The best odds of having kids who don't end up stoned and feckless each and every day is to model sobriety in the home.

None of the above is to suggest that there aren't those who can smoke pot occasionally and function. I have even met a few rare individuals who can smoke pot frequently and still be productive.

But for Racso, it's just not working out.

What the hell was that?

58

Safe at Home

Dr. Val's question slammed me.

My talk at Books & Books in Coral Gables had been progressing smoothly. I was humbled that over a hundred people had taken time out of their full days to come and hear me speak about my first book, <u>Raising Healthy Kids in an Unhealthy World</u>.

My dad had "opened" for me by flawlessly reciting a couple of the dozen poems he knows from memory. My dear friend, Bruce Turkel had eloquently and graciously introduced me. The SRO crowd was laughing in the right places and the live streaming was seamless. In the Q and A, I felt good about my ability to respond to the thoughtful questions from the audience. My main message—"love the kids you get and you'll get the kids you'll love"— seemed to be going over well judging by the smiles and nods. "Take your kids camping," I intoned. "Spend both quality time and quantity time with your beloved children."

What could go wrong?

But then Dr. Val (my colleague from Informed Families) politely asked, "what about families who cannot afford to go on a wilderness trek to Utah. How do these families just be with their children?" The implication was clear: what about a single mom working two jobs? With limited income, she doesn't have the budget for camping gear let alone cross country air tickets. What can she do in the restricted time that she has?

In response, I mumbled something about how my dad and I used to toss a ball back-and-forth in the street in front of our house, that a couple of ball gloves and a baseball are inexpensive. The implication was that even if vacations are outside the budget, modeling appropriate interactions with your kids can happen on the cheap. "Find an hour," I said. "Find an hour each and every day."

With the benefit of perfect hindsight, I find my response inadequate and imperfect. Now that I've had some time to think about it—and now that the cameras are turned off—I want to try to give a better answer. Because the insights for how to raise healthy kids should be similar across neighborhoods, incomes, and social classes.

Just as the best way to increase your odds of surviving the plague in Europe in the Middle Ages was the same regardless of how many chickens a family had.

Half a millennium ago, before an infectious model of disease, before blood borne illnesses were understood, people were dying in droves. Some estimates suggest that one in four people in Europe succumbed. Fleas carried on rats brought by trading ships bit people who got sick and died within days. Indeed, many people believe that one of our oldest nursery rhymes, "Ring around the Rosie," refers to the progression of the disease.

"A rosy rash... was a symptom of the plague, and posies of herbs were carried as protection and to ward off the smell of the disease. Sneezing or coughing was a final fatal symptom, and 'all fall down' was exactly what happened." (Wikipedia.) Most sources discount this connection between the rhyme and the plague.

Families who survived were those who could sequester themselves and avoid infection. Today, keeping our families safe from the dangers of harmful media and process addictions requires similar quarantines. Every family, regardless of income, can "just say no" to screens. Any home can be a safe haven where families read books and talk about ideas rather than focusing on which celebrity married or murdered another.

I will continue to think about Dr. Val's question and how to keep our families safe. In the meantime, here is my improved answer:

Utah need only be as far away as a walk to the public library.

59

Leaf Me Alone?

After mowing the lawn this past Saturday, I discerned that there was yet more yard work to be done at Altshuler Plaza ("where living is a way of life"). Noting that leaves do not typically jump into trash bags on their own, I mentioned to my youngest that perhaps she might join me in my endeavor to keep the photographers from "Worst Kept Home on 62nd Avenue" at bay.

Hobbes may have suggested that life is "solitary, poor, nasty, brutish, and short," but I was determined nonetheless to have company raking leaves. I could be solitary later in the day—when taking the dog for a walk, for example.

My daughter, who had been contentedly watching cartoons, responded to my entreaty regarding leaves specifically and yard work in general with words other than, "Yes, Sir. Right away, Sir."

This was not an answer of which I was enamored.

I reflected on the fact that, although I live with a great number of children, I do entirely too much yard work on my own. I further reflected on the fact that I gave a talk on parenting at Books & Books just the other day. Surely, the man who wrote a book and gave a lecture on parenting SHOULD BE ABLE TO GET HIS 14 YEAR-OLD DAUGHTER TO HELP HIM WITH A LITTLE YARD WORK FOR GOODNESS SAKE WE'RE TALKING ABOUT RAKING A FEW LEAVES HERE NOT THE BATAAN DEATH MARCH.

So, parenting expert that I am, I took the next logical step of entering into a complete and utter psychotic meltdown replete with raving, sputtering, and incoherent four-letter words. The gist of my disconnected shouting may have had something to do with living in a home where people help one another. Admittedly, the logic may have been hard to follow given the number of expletives. I am thankful, given the decibel level of my insane diatribe, that the neighbors did not call the police; I am also thankful that the neighbors did not call the Department of Children and Families to take the first steps toward removing my daughter from my home and promptly placing her in foster care. I continued my frenzied tirade until the youngest of my four kids paused the television, put her sneakers on, and cheerfully joined me in the yard.

Clearly, yelling at a child about living in a happy family where people are nice to each other and help one another with chores is right up there with fighting for peace and f***ing for chastity. Bad plans all. And unlikely to be effective.

After my daughter and I stacked firewood and clipped branches for an hour or two, I had calmed down enough to be pretty much rational. Now that my head was no longer spinning, I apologized. "I'm sorry I yelled at you," I began. "That's no way to treat people."

"It's okay," she replied. We're good."

What am I to make of this comment? "It's okay; we're good." How can a child be so forgiving? Dispensing with hyperbole and humor I will make the following straightforward points:

1) Being a good parent is like running a marathon. It's not about what you do on any one day. It's about what you do year in and year out that matters.

2) Making a mistake and apologizing is better than making a mistake and continuing to be a jerk about it.

3) Making deposits in the Bank of Goodwill with your children allows you to make the occasional withdrawal. Specifically, if you mess up—needlessly screaming at a child, for example—you are more likely to get another chance unless you frequently scream at your child, in which case who would blame her for tuning you out?

4) Making deposits in the Bank of Goodwill is not about allowing your children to play video games and eat ice cream for breakfast. Making deposits is about attending to your children's needs while helping them deal with their wants. ("No you can't have a pony; we live on the 14th floor of a condo with an explicit 'No ponies' policy." But I can certainly appreciate how much you want a pony.")

5) Anyone who thinks that I have the proper insight to each and every question regarding how to raise healthy kids will be brutally disappointed.

But I'm going to keep making the best decisions I can going forward. I'm going to learn from my mistakes. I'm going to do more collaborative problem solving and less authoritarian directing.

I'm going to do less screaming. I hope you will too.

60

Running On

Okay, so I had a little come apart in the Miami marathon in February. Stuff happens. And maybe I should have known better. In retrospect, I guess the clues were fairly abundant. The pasty-looking guy sprawled on the asphalt at Mile 11 might have had something to say had he not been surrounded by a half dozen frenzied paramedics. Had he been able to speak, perhaps he would have mentioned that 87° and high humidity are not optimum conditions for hurling oneself into the void that is 26.2 miles. There was a rumor that 5000 of the people who had signed up for the "fool" marathon did come to appreciate that discretion is the better part of valor and walked—or perhaps, limped—off the course at the half.

Still and all, the professional staff in the medical tent could not have been nicer or more competent. Six bags of ice, one physical therapist on each leg, a bit of psychotic screaming, and one IV glucose bag later, I was up and about, limping toward my loving wife, a hot shower, and a handful of Advil. Apparently, "Barack Obama" was the correct answer to the doctor's inquiry regarding my cognitive capability because I was allowed to leave without being subsequently scheduled for a complete psych eval.

Maybe people weren't meant to run that far comfortably. I don't know. I do know that I can contrast my finishing time of "minor medical emergency" in Miami with The Marathon of the Potomac two weeks ago in which, at mile eight, the following events occurred almost simultaneously:

1) I met a new Best Friend Forever with whom I shared racing stories and life stories over the course of several hours, both of us knowing that we would likely never see or speak to one another again. Melissa has two children—a nine and a three year old—and works for the National Park Service, a lovely person running her fourth marathon.

2) I felt like I could keep running indefinitely. The weather in Northern Virginia was ideal and idyllic, low 50s with a light breeze coming off the river and a shaded course with no traffic. I felt like I had found my "forever pace" and that, as the mellifluous phrase implies, I could run without stopping until the ends of the earth. It is hard to exaggerate or even describe what it is like, at 57 years of age, to feel like you can put your body on cruise control and run for days on end.

Which is not to say that I was unhappy upon reaching the end of the event.

Some people like to go camping with their kids because, after a week on the bumpy ground in the heat, clean sheets and air conditioning are intensely appreciated. The contrast between the experiences heightens the appreciation. Or as Shakespeare put it, "If all the year were playing holidays; To sport would be as tedious as to work."

Both running and camping are reasons why—in case there was any possible doubt—that a birthday party for a six-year-old that includes multiple bounce houses, a train, pony rides, costumed characters performing "Evita", a photo booth, a limo, Margaritas, a pastry chef, and a Keno table are desperately contraindicated. What will the unfortunate child have to look forward to in the future? What can she hope to earn, accomplish, or appreciate if she has been bludgeoned with every conceivable luxury since she started elementary school?

On a recent visit to a residential treatment center, I noticed a half pipe, basketball court, and swimming pool; a music studio with full drum set, guitars, and a professional quality mixing board; and kids creating smoothies with fresh fruit. Students who are making progress in the program were discussing upcoming hiking, rock climbing, and kayaking trips. Students who were not making progress mentioned that in treatment "there is nothing to do here."

None of which is to suggest that loving parents should ignore the needs of children, only that what is meaningful is more likely to be earned rather than given. Hiking a few hours up a rocky trail to a 200-foot waterfall affords a better view then being driven to the same spot. Heck, I could have driven the marathon course but then I wouldn't have met Missy.

Attending to our children's every need while overlooking their wants remains a good plan. Allowing our kids to anticipate achieving and accomplishing on their own is another. Ignoring your own needs—impressing your friends with an over-the-top birthday celebration for a little one, for example— might be the most important gift of all.

61

The Long and Winding Road

Look, nobody is saying that Dorothy had it easy. She had to go a long way round to get back to where she belonged, right? Munchkins, poppies, green horses, were just the beginning. Then that annoying scarecrow telling her to go "both ways"? And don't even get me started about those flying monkeys.

What even my most erudite readers may not know is that a previously unknown manuscript of Frank Baum's hundred year-old story has recently been unearthed—in my very backyard of all places. Can you believe it? I am sure you understand that I am not at liberty to disclose all the details of this archaeological breakthrough which would involve my using phrases including "CIA," "masons," fortuitous coincidences," "manuscript sniffing German shepherds," and "none of this ever actually happened." Though Baum's last draft is incomplete, here are a few of the paragraphs that have been deciphered:

Scene: Castle interior. Stone walls festooned with torches, mold, and pennants of highly competitive colleges.

Wicked Witch: Take organic chemistry next year, my pretty.

Dorothy: Have you read <u>Pride and Prejudice</u>? Don't you just adore Jane Austen? I want to read and study everything she's written.

Wicked Witch: what would you do with an English major, teach? (Derisive cackle.)

Dorothy: I have always found peace working with charcoal and pastels. I wonder if I could find my true passion with acrylics or oils.

Wicked Witch: go to medical school! (Hurls flaming fireball.)

Dorothy: I barely got a B- in pre-calculus and I studied three hours every day. Math comes hard for me.

Wicked Witch: All the careers and big starting salaries are in computer science! Studying art history is a waste of time and money!

Dorothy: there's no place like Rome. There's no place like Rome.

As I mentioned, not all the pages of this classic have been discovered. The search for the complete manuscript. continues. Where will the complete text be found? Is it possible that indeed more of this very conversation is going on in the present day in your home?

Are you encouraging your child—"forcing" is such an ugly word—to study that which she neither enjoys nor for which she has any discernible aptitude?

My gentle sarcasm is not a narrow argument in favor of students favoring the liberal arts over science, technology, engineering, and mathematics. To the contrary, I am virulently in favor of all academic disciplines from anthropology to zoology. My point is simply that for many students choosing to study biochemistry rather than history is a false dichotomy. Students who excel in both disciplines can make an informed choice. More common are students who can do well in some majors or fail in others.

My long-standing and favorite dictum, "love the children you get and you'll get the children you love" can be shortened: let them be who they are. And at the risk of extending this metaphor, you want to be the parent who is attuned to your child's needs. You do not want to be the tornado that rips your child away from where she needs to be, from the place to which she will invariably and rightfully return.

You don't need to discover a manuscript in your backyard to have contented children and peace in your home. Flying monkeys are more likely to enforce compliance than to solidify a loving relationship.

62

The Muck Stops Here

Remember reading about those brutally mistreated Chinese girls of not so many generations ago whose feet were bound with strong straps? For reasons that may not even have been clear at the time, fathers felt that petite feet were attractive or indicative of a social class where the girls didn't have to walk much. Maybe the fathers were happy that their injured daughters couldn't run away and go to medical school. The crippled girls, in needless, constant pain, were perhaps less happy.

Apparently, woman with three-inch feet were considered attractive. If you read the Wikipedia Article, you'll know as much about bound feet as I do.

Before affecting horror and outrage at another culture and another century, reflect on a frequent series of inquiries that my college counseling colleagues and I encounter from families who want their daughters to attend "top" colleges. After 34 years of counseling, college admissions is a subject that I do profess to know something about.

Dad: We don't want to game the system. (Translation: We want to game the system.)

Dad: We don't want you to confer an unfair advantage. (Translation: Could you make a few calls?)

Dad: We just want to know how much of her time should be allocated to playing soccer, running for student counsel, editing the student newspaper, building robots, playing the bouzouki, hang gliding, Cotillion lessons, and volunteering at the Whoop Kitchen.

Ethical College Counselors Everywhere: Surely, you mean the "soup" kitchen?

Dad: No, all the positions at the soup kitchen were taken so our daughter cheers and hollers for the girls who do the actual serving. "Way to go! Serve that soup!" That sort of thing. She gets the same number of community service hours though so it doesn't matter.

ECCE: Doesn't matter to whom?

Dad: Sometimes she tries to fall asleep when she studies after all these activities but my wife and I poke her with a stick to keep her awake and focused.

ECCE: You poke your daughter with a stick so she can stay awake and study after being involved in all those time consuming activities after school?

Dad: Yes, we tried hooking her up to an IV glucose solution when her energy ran low, but her arm got infected from the needle sticks.

ECCE: Her arm got infected?

Dad: She plays soccer. Weren't you listening? Her arms don't matter; the girls kick the soccer ball with their feet.

We want to give her the best chance of being admitted to a top college where she will likely meet a man who can provide for her in the fashion to which we insist that she continue to be accustomed.

ECCE: Which of those activities is she passionate about?

Dad: none of them, really. She likes art. Why do you ask?

After listening to this dad, is the analogy with the tortuously bound feet seeming a little less outrageous?

And what guesses would you make about this young woman's relationship with her father down the road—whether or not she achieves his dream of being admitted to a top college and marrying a wealthy man?

But shouldn't children work hard, strive for the best, listen to their parents, and do what they're told?

I don't know. I do know that if I had to choose, I'd rather have a content child than a successful one. Fortunately, I don't have to choose. Kids who are allowed to follow their own path and "be who they are" are more likely to succeed by every meaningful definition of the word.

I met a high achieving young woman just the other day as it happens. Four AP classes as a tenth grader, star or her traveling soccer team, high test scores. I met her in a rehab facility I was touring in Northern Utah. The young woman had become addicted to meth amphetamine.

I know. I know. Using one example and even hinting that there is a causal connection between the high pressure and the drug use is a cheap shot. Yes, there are pressured kids who succeed just as there are low achieving kids who also turn to drugs. Using just the one child to make a point is a lousy technique of crumby political campaigns not a strategy I should use in this thoughtful book.

But that young woman's accomplishments in the classroom contrasted with her struggles on the street really hit home for me.

Before you tell me that there are evils and stressors in the world to which our children must be exposed and that our kids need to be able to deal successfully with stress, let me remind you that there are carcinogens in the world but the existence of these toxins is a poor argument for sending your children to soccer camp at the site of a nuclear disaster.

Speaking of disasters, I would be grateful for your insights into how to counsel dads like the one (only slightly exaggerated) above. In the meantime, I'm going to go back to focusing on how to best love my kids for who they are—not for what grades they get, what activities they're involved in, where they go to college, or whether or not they have small feet.

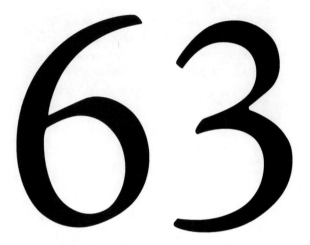

Match Game

I don't want to give too many details. I'm not saying this is a good idea what I did, only that it can happen. I know it can happen and how it happened because I did it. I'm not saying that I would want anyone to follow this exact path or that it was a good idea and I guess maybe I cut some corners. I suppose you could say that what I did was wrong.

It started when I was a high school athlete. Again without being too specific, let's just say my dad knew the coach. I'm not saying influence was involved; I'm not saying it wasn't. Anyway, I got to be on the football team instead of some other guys who maybe had a little more ability or worked a little harder.

I guess college was a similar circumstance. I made the team at a Division One school. Sure there were other guys who were faster, stronger, more experienced, and better players all around. But sometimes you have to do what you have to do.

The end justifies the means, right? So I sent the coach some videotapes that have me running 40 yards in 4.2 seconds. And I got a doctor to sign off on my being able to bench press 225 pounds 37 times. Maybe the doctor owed my dad a favor. The tape wasn't exactly accurate. Forty yards in 4.2 seconds may have been something of an exaggeration. It is no exaggeration to say that I took every human growth hormone, steroid, injection and illegal performance enhancing drug I could find. I hired a doctor to give me some other drugs so that the illegal drugs couldn't be detected.

Again, I don't want to give away too many of the details. Let's just say that I was drafted to play in the NFL and made the team. Through some fairly sophisticated subterfuge, I got through training camp. I used a stunt double and I talked my way through some stuff with the coaches who relied on my fake videos and some other tricky stuff.

So now the first game is in a few minutes and I'm thinking about how I've never actually played any football. I'll be lining up opposite Randy Stark. He's the 6'3", 305 pound starting defensive tackle for the Miami Dolphins. He actually can do 37 bench press repeats at 225 pounds. Actually, he's kind of a beast. The truth of the matter is that I am 5' 10" and weigh 175 pounds.

How do you think I'm going to do against Randy Stark in the game?

***

Laura's parents really, truly, and desperately want her to attend the California Institute of technology. That's where they both went, where they meant. Laura's parents are willing to do anything for her to go there. Her parents believe strongly that Laura's best chance of meeting a man who will be successful is by attending Caltech. Laura's grades are above average, although she is struggling in her senior year of math, pre-calculus. She has friends—some of whom are also applying to Cal Tech—who are two years ahead of her in math and are sailing through advanced placement calculus BC. A few of her friends, also still in high school, are taking differential equations at the University. Laura has a 580 on the SAT. The main SAT score for matriculating students at Cal Tech is some 200 points higher. Laura reluctantly studies an hour and a half each day. Most students at Cal Tech study over three and half hours each day. Laura is reluctant to meet with the tutors whom her parents have hired.

Still, let's say that Laura is admitted. Her parents contribute ten million dollars or fake her transcript or there's a computer glitch or some crazy thing and she gets the "Congratulations" email rather than the "We had too many qualified applicants" one. (I'm asking for a little willing suspension of disbelief here, just like in the implausible football story above.)

Were Laura, with her modest math ability, study skills, attitude, and aptitude, to be admitted to Cal Tech, how well do you think she might be expected to do in a classroom filled with smarter, harder working students? I would suggest that the metaphor of the 175-pound man described above who somehow scammed his way into a professional football uniform is an accurate representation in every particular of how Laura is going to do if she goes to Pasadena.

Metaphorically, Laura is going to have every bone in her body shattered.

The point of going to college isn't just to get in; the point of going to college is to stay in. And learn something while you're there. And to study hard and thrive, not just survive. And to go to the art museum on campus and sit down with a professor so you can share a meal, a book, and an idea.

"College admissions is about a match to be made not a game to be won" remains true throughout my 30-something years in the field.

The take-away for parents is simple and straightforward: Know who your kids are. And love them anyway. If your kid belongs at Cal Tech, encourage her to apply and celebrate her choice if she is admitted. If your kids don't belong at Cal Tech—and with room for just under a thousand undergraduates, most kids don't—be happy for them where ever they end up.

Helping your kids to scam their resumes, inflate their accomplishments, and be admitted to schools where they don't belong is as ill-advised as helping a 5" 10", 175-pound man line up in an NFL game against Randy Starks: a true recipe for sadness.

On the field and in the classroom, there is nothing worse than a bad match.

64

Allo!

My family and I enjoyed hosting Cornelius, a 15 year-old exchange student from Northern France, once we got over our nagging concern that we did indeed have the right child from the right country. "They all speak English fluently," my thoughtful wife was told at the orientation meeting at the school. "Perfectly." My wife even wrote down the word "perfectly" so that she wouldn't forget and so that she could impress on me that Cornelius wouldn't be a problem to communicate with during his stay.

"What's one more kid?" I agreed. "Two weeks is fine."

Of course, as anyone who has ever watched congressional hearings can attest, sometimes the most simple, straightforward concepts can be the squirmiest to pin down. Cornelius was most certainly able to communicate a few critical phrases including "Allo!" and "I not understood" but was lost with some of the more abstract concepts that we throw around in our erudite home. The words for "chicken," "fork," and "vegetable," for example, were all beyond his imperfect proficiency. And I shudder to think what might have happened had the concept of dividing fractions come up in conversation at the dinner table

Of course even Cornelius's stumbling English was superior to my limited ability to communicate in French. Indeed, I only know a few words and, as there seemed no reason for me to mention either "Dom Perignon" or "Bridgette Bardot," conversation was necessarily limited. "Allo!" Cornelius would brightly greet me several times each day. "Invert the denominator and multiply" I was tempted to respond.

Finally the children gracelessly pointed out what they had known all along: our smart phones were smarter than we and could translate impeccably from French to English and back again. After this discovery, we all had a pretty good time. I don't remember the French words for "volleyball," "canoe," and "Dairy Queen" but the visit seemed to work out pretty well and the two weeks passed quickly.

Which brings me—"finally," you might say—to my insight about parenting for this week.

How would you know if what you were saying to your kids wasn't being 'heard'? How would you know if you might as well be speaking a foreign language? Remember what Charlie Brown hears when the teacher speaks in the televised cartoons? "Wah, wah, wah, wah, wah." How do you know that when you say, "How was your day at school?" that your child doesn't hear, "Wah, wah, wah, wah, wah"?

One clear indication might be getting an answer that you can't translate--even with your smart phone--or that you know not to be true. Everybody knows the terrible joke about the guy who makes a "Freudian Slip" at dinner: His mother says, "Please pass the potatoes" and he responds, 'You ruined my life, you f***ing wrench.'"

When you ask your kids every day what their grades are and they say they're doing fine but you know darn well that their grades are not at all what you would prefer, maybe what they're trying to say is "I not understood." There is certainly a serious disconnect somewhere.

More gently put, if you're asking your kids how they're doing in school and the answers don't make sense, ie, "Everything's great" or "we didn't have any homework and anyway I already did it," maybe you're not asking the right questions.

Maybe you're not even speaking the same language.

65

Control Leak

I don't know what happened on December 6, 1941. I don't know what led up to all that unpleasantness between the Hatfields and the McCoys. I don't even want to think about what happened between you and your ex in the years leading up to the dissolution of your marriage.

I do know that the Mad Magazine headline—"Mom gives birth to teenager; no telling what these kids will do next"—notwithstanding, there is always a day before when it comes to kids. They don't arrive, like Athena born fully grown out of the brain of Zeus, as oppositional, defiant, snarky, non-communicative, sneaky, unpleasant high schoolers. You don't need a Master's in Developmental Psychology (aka "home economics with numbers") to know that infants become babies who turn into toddlers who go to kindergarten before starting middle school and pretending not to hear when asked repeatedly to take out the garbage.

I've written a lot about how hard it is to raise healthy kids in this toxic culture. The ubiquitous dangers of process addictions—drugs, alcohol, video games, gambling, and Internet pornography—are familiar themes in these chapters. The first thing I try to do for the lost parents of out-of-control teens is to assure them that they didn't create the problems in their homes and communities all by themselves. The parents of an angry, depressed, anxious, acting-out, pot smoking tenth grader who refuses to go to school ask me what they did wrong. I tease mom by inquiring if she is an Afghan drug lord responsible for importing tons of heroin into our country. I joke with dad about whether he is guilty of inventing the billion dollar video gaming industry that is designed to keep children playing frenetically. I am convinced that the first step to healing for parents is to understand that they themselves are not wholly responsible for their children's issues.

Because nothing is worse than the blame heaped upon the parents of children with "problems." If your kid doesn't look a stranger in the eye and say, "Nice to meet you, Sir," it is the parents who are thought to have failed to instruct their child in proper behavior. If your one-year-old isn't sleeping through the night, if your three-year-old isn't sitting still on an airplane, if your tenth grader isn't taking four AP courses and acing them all, somehow you, the parent, are at fault. Somehow you managed to take time off from hiding Jimmy Hoffa's body to also irreversibly mess up your child.

The logical outcome of the pointed fingers and whispered remarks about your misbehaved child is that YOU SHOULD HAVE BEEN MORE CONTROLING. "Spare the rod and spoil the child." "If my father had acted like that, my grandfather would have knocked half his teeth out before whipping him with a belt." "In the old days, children were seen and not heard."

Well, in the old days a cure for many medical ailments was to allow leeches to suck blood from the ailing patient. Women were routinely tortured and burned for having caused the crops to die. The "old days" may have had advantages—the absence of reality TV shows springs readily to mind—but our understanding of how to raise healthy children wasn't among them.

There is tremendous pressure on families in this generation to have their children COMPLY. Power and control issues are rampant in families and reaching epidemic proportions in the culture. The academic pressure on kids is unbearable. (If I may speak frankly, I'd like to see YOU study successfully for three AP classes as a junior after coming home from rowing practice having gotten only five hours of sleep the night before.) Parents ask me all the time how to get their children to study more. I try to redirect the conversation: what would happen if your children were to study LESS? How can we tone down the risk of your kids turning to drugs to self-medicate? Is there more than one way to define success?

"Let them be who they are" and "love your kids for who they are, not what they do" are my recurrent themes. The other side of the argument is to try to force your kids to comply with vacuous rules that will doubtless look ill-advised in a generation or two. Just as every rational person is aghast at leeches as medicine and burning of witches, historians a few decades hence will be horrified at how parents in 2014 tried to control their children. The lack of compliance and the rampant drug use of our kids are due, in no small part, to how much their parents obsess over their every move, action, thought, and high school course selection.

What happened the day before your daughter started cutting herself? What happened the day before she started smoking pot morning, noon, and night? What happened the day before your son refused to go to school for the first time?

It is possible that you have been telling your kids how to behave in so many trivial ways that they are unable to distinguish that what is practically meaningless—finish your spelling homework, for example—from that which is life threatening: stay away prescription painkillers?

The time to start relinquishing control is now. Because today could very well be the day before it's too late.

Cui Bono?

No, not Sonny and Cher's lesser known relative. Cui Bono is Latin for "who benefits?" Whose interests are served? Throughout your children's development, keeping this query uppermost in your mind in your every interaction with them will make your kids more likely to grow up to be content, fulfilled, and self actualized. As a result you, the loving parent, will be less likely to want to put a fork in your eye.

The following endlessly repetitive examples will drive this critical point deep into your heart. (Yes, there is probably a better metaphor that doesn't evoke images of Vlad the Impaler. No, I can't think of it just now.) Are you correcting your child's behavior to make your child happy or to make yourself happy? To be fair, I will give examples of both when it is in your child's interest for you to insist on a behavior as well as examples when you should probably back off.

1) Potty training: Yes. Insist on it. Everyone benefits. Remember when you thought the penny was never going to drop? The parent of an older child assured you that your child "won't walk down the aisle in diapers"? They were right. I am going to come right out and say that the Anti-Potty Training Lobby gets no support from me.

2) Choice of College Major: Studying literature rather than accounting or choosing accounting rather than literature. Not so much. If you are an accountant, imagine being forced to read Moby Dick. In Latin. All day. Conversely, if you love books, consider what it would be like to look constantly at balance sheets and then find the square root. Encouraging your kids to have a bite of the baked talapia is one thing. Forcing raw eels down their throats is another. Let them choose what they want to study. Stated another way: let them be who they are.

3) Marriage: Should you allow your daughter to marry Lee whom she prefers rather than Robin, the one you think will be better for her? Look, I don't like Lee any more than you do. If you must know, he still owes me $200 and, maybe I shouldn't bring this up just now, but I'm still not exactly comfortable with what happened to my mom's silver teapot that has been missing ever since the last time he was over here for Thanksgiving. Just the same, SHE seems to love him. Leave it alone. Walk away.

4) Dieting: If your love for your wife allows you to encourage her to lose weight because of your concern for her cardiovascular well-being, you are less likely to spend the rest of your life sleeping on the couch than if you want her to shed a few pounds so that you won't be embarrassed at the company pick-nick. Similarly, love and concern over your child's healthy eating habits are easier to sell than raving about whether or not she'll ever get a date because she makes a beeping noise when she backs up. Did it ever occur to you that maybe she doesn't WANT to date just now? Can you live with that? Because I take her at her word, that she'll date when she's ready. Why can't you believe her?

Even a stray dog knows whether it has been tripped over or kicked.

Nobody wants to be controlled.

As contradictory as it sounds, the more choices you allow your children to make for themselves when they're younger, the more likely they are to make the choices that you would like them to make subsequently. Sure you can force them to study accounting and marry Robin (believe me, he's no prize either), but ultimately all they're going to learn is, well, force. For modeling— the most powerful teaching tool of all—to work, you have to love your kids for who they are rather than for what they do. Your kids are kinda pre-programmed to like you. The cherry on top is recusing yourself from telling them what to do each and every solitary moment of the day year in year out on and on into infinity.

London's longest-running musical, "The Fantasticks, "had over 17,000 performances. Neither "Les Mis" nor "Phantom" each with 11,000 performances, comes close. Could part of "The Fantastics" enduring popularity have been because it expressed this truth as follows?

Why did the kids pour jam on the cat?
Raspberry jam all over the cat?
Why should the kids do something like that,
When all that we said was no?

In summary: Let the kids make decisions—good and bad—when they're young to avoid subsequent sticky felines.

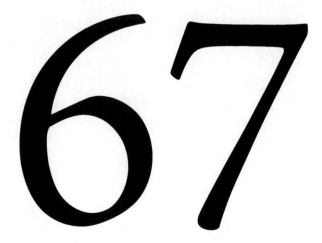

For Whom

No, this column isn't a lesson about objective case pronouns; it's about some of the best parenting I've ever seen:

Twenty-something years ago, my eight-week-old first born had just nodded off. After placing her in the new crib, my friend and I watched Jolie sleep, her tiny body breathing rhythmically. If there is anything more glorious than watching an infant nap, I cannot imagine what that experience might be. My buddy started to lean over to kiss the baby, but stopped. "No," she said. "That would be for me, not for her."

My loving friend wanted to display her affection; but my two-month-old baby needed to rest undisturbed. My contemporary wanted one more brush of that magical "baby touch." But my little one needed her afternoon snooze. Whose needs are primary? Yes, this is a rhetorical question. Obviously the needs of the child must always come first.

Or do they? Do you, for example, endlessly tell your kids how smart they are? If so, whose interests are being served? I suspect I know you're thinking: You want your child to have a good sense of herself. You want her to know that she can do anything. You want her to feel capable.

Or do you just want to feel good about yourself because having a smart child reflects well on you?

Let me ask you something: has anyone ever convinced you to change your opinion of yourself based on a comment-no matter how often the same words were repeated?

Kids feel good about their ability to make fires not from being <u>told</u> that they know how to build fires. Seeing the flames resulting from the proper placement of kindling is what works. Kids feel good about their ability to perform well in school from actually doing well in school, not from being told that they can. Indeed, recent research suggests that focusing on a child's motivation rather than her capacity makes sense. Kids who feel their good performance comes from trying hard will be more likely to try hard. Kids who feel that their results come only from their aptitude have less reason to stick to a project and see it through to success. And, as we all know, hard work almost always trumps innate ability. But I digress.

What about your need to see you child go to the best college? Again, I can anticipate your good thoughts: Kids who go to "top" colleges end up being admitted to graduate schools and going on to live happy, wealthy lives. But let's see if there aren't gaping holes in this line of reasoning: what if kids who go to "top" colleges were "top" kids to begin with? What if plenty of kids from North Cornstalk State Drooling University end up in medical school just the same? Could your intense—"psychotic" and "delusional" are such ugly words—desire to see your daughter at a top college be more about your need to be perceived as a successful parent rather than about what your child needs? Maybe your child needs to go to a school where she can be a big fish in a small pond. Maybe she doesn't have the horses (ability) or the whip (motivation) to be successful at a college that routinely turns down kids with perfect SATs who were graduated first in their high school classes. Would you still love your child were she to end up at a "lesser" school? And yes, I'm hoping that's a rhetorical question too.

So the question is always: "Who benefits?" Or more grammatically: "For whom is this?" If the kisses are FOR the baby, then kiss the baby. But if the kisses are to remind you that you are a loving parent, let the baby sleep. If the choice of college is about where your child will thrive in a productive way, then go ahead and apply to "top" schools rather than to North Cornstalk.

Just keep in uppermost in your mind who your child is and how her needs will best be met.

68

What's in a Label?

Standing around the kitchen of a buddy of mine who had recently received a $350,000 MacArthur Genius Grant for his lifetime achievements in the field of poetry, it occurred to the few remaining guests that there are only so many ways to say "congratulations" and even fewer ways to say "Man, that is a LOT of money for writing poems" and so it was time to clean up some plates and cups before heading back to our Non-Genius-Award lives. Even big celebrations at this stage of life involve more half-eaten bagels than empty wine bottles, so there were more plates than glasses to deal with. After watching the MacArthur recipient struggle unsuccessfully for some minutes to negotiate the placement of a bowl in the dishwasher rack, his wife took the pewter object from him, placed it effortlessly in the machine, and remarked, "yeah, he's a genius."

Yet my topic this week is not about "all kinds of minds" and how we should allow our children to excel in those areas in which they have aptitude and enjoyment rather than berate them endlessly regarding those areas where they lack skill. Nor is my screed on these pages about how, had Thomas been forced to master "Dish Placement" before moving on to literature, our world would be a poorer place. Instead, I want to examine my own label, that of "mental health professional." Do I possess enough mental health to be considered stable, never mind in possession of enough of said quantity to dispense it to others? Is my buddy a genius just because he got an award for $350K? Am I qualified to give advice about how to bring up healthy kids just because I—er, well—give advice about how to bring up healthy kids?

So, to determine my status, I performed the following assessment: I took my precious six-year-old daughter and our equally adorable brown dog outside where we proceeded to stand for some time, waiting to cross the busy street on which we live. Needless to say, no car stopped to let our intrepid party proceed. Indeed, no car slowed down. It could be argued that no driver looked away from simultaneously applying makeup, drinking coffee, changing the CD, and talking on the phone to notice our minor plight. My mental health question is this: how angry is it appropriate to be, not being able to traverse the street in front of my own house with my daughter and dog?

Clearly, I am fortunate beyond reason to even live in a house; few people in the world do. I am not addressing my sense of entitlement nor am I thinking about one of my old students who, at the ripe old age of 35, sold some software to AOL for tens of millions of dollars and retired—doubtless to a less busy street. No, my question is simply this: how angry is it appropriate to be that no driver in this town will stop to allow a child and a dog to cross a street? If I am indeed a mental health professional, my mental health should not be negatively affected by standing with my daughter and our dog on the curb for a few interminable minutes waiting to cross the street as cars speed obliviously by.

Or should it?

What about the fact that I was here first? I was born and bred in this town. I have lived in Miami for 58 years and paid prodigious taxes for most of those years. Who are all these tourists? Don't you agree that they've got their nerve coming down here from the tundra of New Jersey driving on the street where I have lived for generations? And what about common courtesy? And what about the fact that they're all watching movies and writing novels while driving, not paying attention to children and dogs on the side of the road at all?

Ah. Now we're getting somewhere. Because my annoyance at not being able to take my daughter and our dog for a walk is based on deeper issues, issues that have nothing to do with what I originally said they have to do with. My annoyance—now solidly a 17 on a scale of one to ten—isn't about the infinitely rude drivers at all.

So now, let me ask you: when you gently and politely inquire as to whether or not you're able bodied, healthy, 17-year-old son will put away the laundry that you were gracious enough to wash, dry, fold and leave in a basket outside his door after only being asked 47 times, are you just annoyed—as you could very well be—or is there an underpinning feeling of not being valued? Or are you concerned about a future in which your son continues his slovenly ways and ends up drinking wine in the gutter as a result? Are you perhaps pissed at your ex-husband who never helped with the laundry either?

When you tell your son to do his homework, is there a resonance for you relating to your son's academic future or lack of one? Do you catastrophize in a way that your son does not?

Gentle, directed advice for this week: when you feel yourself getting angry with your kids, S-T-O-P and ask yourself the question: why am I so intensely and thoroughly ticked off? If the answer has more to do with yourself and less to do with the kids, it just might be time to take a break. Might I recommend taking the family dog for a walk? You can cross the street here, right in front of my house.

69

Could it Be this Simple?

A number of my gentle readers have inquired regarding my modeling advice. Not "Wear nice clothes to the audition," modeling. Parents want to know how to combat the snares of process addictions by modeling appropriate behaviors. They want to know how to help their kids love reading (could it be as simple as just reading to them?) and avoid video games (is it as straight forward as just staying off the computer?) Moms and dads want to know how to bring up healthy kids in a toxic culture.

We get it, they say. Stop screaming at the kids; stop trying to change them; love them for who they are not for what they do.

But just the same, they go on, We'd still like to have our kids get off the darn X-box and pick up a book just this once. We'd like them to be successful. And while we know many folks who have jobs that require reading, we seldom see want ads including the phrase "must be able to play 'Call of Duty' for hours on end rather than interacting with any actual humans."

I could not agree more. Or as my grandmother used to say, "Rich or poor, it's good to have money." Of course, we want our kids to grow up to be independent and self-supporting. There is hardly a more frighteningly cogent image than that of a 30 year-old living in your basement, emerging only to get more Cheez Doodles and ask to borrow your credit card "just this one last time."

So we are agreed that nothing succeeds like success. The question remains how to help our kids get from sleeping on the corner of Sloth Street and Feckless Avenue over to walking proudly down Independence Boulevard. Clearly, yelling is contraindicated. Absent "Look out! The crosstown bus is about to knock you into the middle of next week!" yelling at kids just teaches them to be yellers themselves.

So here's my four-step process:

1) No video games. You heard it here first. You wouldn't leave narcotics out in the open, not even if "all the other kids [are] doing it." Books, sunshine, Frisbees, mud, trees, yes. Walking the family dog, making brownies, planting trees, fixing bikes, making campfires? Also yes. Computer games? Absolutely not. Why take a chance with something so powerful with so much capacity for harm? The five most powerful words of parenting are "Let's go toss a ball."

2) Note the intensity of the commitment to "being there" with your kids. Yes, I heard about those absent English fathers who trucked their six year-old progeny off to boarding school only to have their handsome, erudite kids return to the manor a decade later ready to defend the empire.

But I never met any.

3) Attunement. Hopefully your kids will show up from the factory grooving on anything brightly colored moving object and you can roll a big plastic ball back and forth with your six year-old before blinking your eyes and going outside to have a catch with your 16 year-old who now throws better than you. But not all kids are ball kids and Ferdinand the Bull might show up in the maternity ward instead. (For those of you who somehow missed Munro Leaf's delicious 1938 book, The Story of Ferdinand, I will only whet your desire by mentioning that Ferdinand would rather smell flowers than participate in bull fights. Not that I blame him.) If your kid would rather

build space ships with dad and Legos rather than toss the pigskin, that's okay too.

4) Then "love them for who they are rather than what they do."

Because you did what you could do.

And they are who they are.

70

So it Has Come to This

Theresa 's 11th grade transcript was admirable: Advanced Placement courses in chemistry, American History, and English each with a grade of A. Her SATs were strong, her ACTs even stronger. Although she was uncomfortable about her extra-curriculars—endless hours volunteering as a math tutor—I was able to reassure her that even were she a bouzouki player or captain of the underwater rugby team that admission to "top" schools is never a slam dunk and that her profile put her "in the pot." That is to say, she had about an 8% chance of being admitted to schools that admit about 8% of their applicants.

Before I could even attempt to assuage her anxiety further, by explaining that "Dartmouth or Die" is a no-win way of walking through the transition process, her dad spoke up. He was concerned—"frenetic" is harder for me to spell—about his daughter's grade point average. Theresa's unweighted 3.7 weighed heavily on his soul. He explained how his daughter had taken two courses at North Cornstalk State, the local community college, but had received Bs in both. "Our strategy exploded horribly," he explained.

Unable to perceive any shrapnel or shattered lives in my office, I tried to massage the conversation around to learning rather than credentialing, Silly me. I inelegantly inquired whether Theresa had enjoyed her advanced courses at the college—her Bs notwithstanding.

All three family members went nacoleptically silent. "What courses did you take?" I blundered on. "You're an advanced math student. Having taken all the courses—BC calculus and AP statistics—that your high school has to offer, did you go on to differential equations at the college?"

After glancing at her parents, Theresa spoke up: "I took introductory Spanish and an algebra I course."

Pushing my befuddled foot still deeper into my gaping mouth, I continued, "But you have native fluency in Spanish and you mastered the algebra I curriculum three years ago."

Again, the family was loudly silent. Had I asked them to do the chicken dance? Did somebody die? Finally Theresa's dad spoke up. "We had heard that admissions to top schools depends on grade point average. So we loaded up on courses where she was sure to get As."

Like Wile E. Coyote who runs off the edge of the cliff but hasn't yet looked down, I still wasn't getting it. Fortunately, dad continued: "But her Spanish teacher found out that Theresa speaks Spanish, so he refused to give her more than a B. And the math teacher did not grade fairly either. Do you think that's just? Why should she be penalized for that which she already knows?"

What isn't fair, I thought to myself, is that this child is being treated like a product rather like an actual human teenager. What isn't fair is that this family is trying to game the system. What isn't fair is that this child views her entire education only as a means to an end.

Can you imagine a native speaker sitting through endless repetitions of "Hola, Paco, como esta?"

Just to pad a transcript which, from the look of it, didn't need any padding? But if the purpose of sending this kid to the community college to sit through courses from which she could not possibly learn anything was to communicate to Theresa 1) that she wasn't okay as she was and 2) that admissions is a game to be played not a match to be made, then perhaps she got that message loudly and clearly.

***

Look, I'm not a zealot. I don't spend weekday mornings in the park slobbering about how a child will learn more from reading an actual book than from doing yet another vapid worksheet. I don't drone on about how the agenda in many high schools is about power and control rather than learning that which might be intrinsically motivating, beautiful, or even—perish forbid!—useful. Although I have been known to give a student or two a book or two over the years, I am not one of those "outside agitators" referenced in "The Graduate."

Clearly, earning $60,000 a year is "better" in every meaningful definition of the word than earning $40,000, don't you agree? You can buy more food with the extra twenty thousand dollars and not worry so much about finances. But is earning $60,000,000 a year so much more important than earning $40,000,000? Don't you think you could somehow manage to stumble through a year with a lousy $40M? How much is enough? What is the cost of that extra money? What is the value of that extra .1 of gpa?

A 3.8 rather than a 3.7 unweighted gpa doesn't significantly affect Theresa's admissibility at "top" schools or harm her in any way. But viewing her education as something that is done to her over which she has no control does not do her any good. There has got to be something wrong about a bilingual kid listening endlessly to "Muy bien, y tu?"

71

Let Me Not Always See the Same Hands

Would you sell your 14 year-old daughter to marauders for $20 so you could score some drugs to support your careening habit? Of course not. Your child is less likely to be accepted to law school never mind live a contented life if she is employed as a forced sex worker overseas. Full marks for ticking the "and anyway I'm not a crack head" box.

Next Question: would you insist that your daughter marry the abusive, drunken scion of the wealthy landowner whose acreage adjoins your own ancestral fiefdom? Even if you needed money to pay back your looming gambling debts?

Well done if you chose, "do I LOOK like the Earl of Trockenheim?" from among the answers. Of course my daughter can marry whom she chooses even if he is not landed gentry.

Question Three: Would you push your daughter ahead in school, make her start when she was four years old rather than five? Because you were tired of doing the parent thing? Because you need to get the crops in?

A+ if you remembered that you haven't actually lived on a farm in several generations.

Question Four: After an arduous rowing season replete with 5:00 am practices, weightlifting, running, and endless hours on the water, your daughter does not "make weight" for the finals. Without her knowledge, do you grab her pony and lop it off with a rusty machete so that she drop that last half pound and compete?

Good for you if you said that the majority of the emergency hair cut decision should remain with the person attached to said hair.

And lastly: What do you do when you hear your baby crying? Do you think, "How is she going to learn to comfort herself if we're constantly cuddling, comforting, and changing her?" When your husband gets up at 2:00 am, do you admonish him by saying: "It's an ugly world out there. Do you imagine for one minute that the United States Senate Subcommittee is going to be sensitive and nurturing when they are asking her questions about the culpability of her troops in a foreign insurrection?"

All the right answers can be summarized with the following two simple precepts: 1) err on the side of agency, that is, letting your daughter make her own decision. Gentle guidance and suggestion? Yes. Grabbing her from behind and cutting off her hair? Not so much. 2) Err on the side of nurture.

That way, on the rare occasion when you do have to enforce your will on your kids (inoculations against measles, mumps, and rubella, for example) you will be thought of as that large person who has your child's interests at heart, who helps them figure things out, who wants what is best for them, not as that Fascist jailer person who is always forcing them to do stuff.

Otherwise, it's hard for the kids to distinguish where they end and where you begin.

Last scenario: Your 14 year-old daughter has amassed forty dollars babysitting for the snarky, high energy, pre-school twins down the street. She wants to use her hard earned samoleans to purchase a "my little pony" a.k.a.

239

overpriced, plastic, worthless piece of garbage that will break in five minutes anyway and-here's the worst of it—GIVE said overpriced, piece of junk to the very four-year-olds from whose parents she received the money in the first place when you and I both know that those kids won't be appreciative for a New York second and obviously that money would be better spent on books and school supplies or invested and what about the college fund and who does she think she is making such an ill-advised purchasing decision? (Whew!)

Should you refuse to drive her to the store explaining in no uncertain terms why it is inappropriate to throw away her money on such a poor choice of gift and worse choice of recipient? Or should you-after a brief explanation of your thoughts—allow her to make a small mistake at a young age to help her avoid larger mistakes subsequently?

Because the step from choosing a plastic toy to choosing a college, career, or husband is shorter than can possibly be imagined. And—as counter-intuitive as it sounds—the less you force her to do things now, the less you'll want to force her to do things later.

The history of parenting is a march from treating our kids as property—farm hands, chattel—to viewing our children as the greatest gift of all, to be valued immeasurably and loved unconditionally.

72

It's about Time

Gathering at the hearth predates the Internet by 800,000 years. Gathering at the hearth predates communicating with symbols by 550,000 years. Gathering at the hearth predates an evolutionary adaptive increase in brain size by 300,000 years.

Before you were you, before your ancestors had evolved into a species that could charitably be mistaken for human, even before you first listened to James Taylor's "Fire and Rain" you were gathering at the hearth and sharing a meal. You think finding all those receipts and getting your taxes done takes forever? Please. You have no idea. Evolving from Homo ergaster to Homo sapiens, now THAT took some time.

Not that there was much else to do, mind you, what with both discotheques and the Kardashians 4/5 of a million years down the road. What were you and your kith and kin doing gathering around the hearth? Were you waiting for the 787 Dreamliner to be invented so you could split from sub-Sahara

Africa and check out who was playing at Madison Square Garden? No. What you were doing was you were sharing food.

That's it. There wasn't much else to do. Stone tools were several hundred generations down the evolutionary trail. There was no point in calling your Realtor to see if your condo had sold because, let's face it, nobody was going to buy your condo.

Gathering at the hearth is what you did not only because there was nothing else to do (You think your kids are bored on a rainy Saturday morning <u>now</u>?) but also because it was the right call. In what is sometimes referred to as the anthropomorphic principle, those other guys, the ones who didn't gather at the hearth and share food hoping that someone would hurry up and invent language so that they could tell the story of the talking dog? Those guys didn't make it. They didn't gather at the hearth and share food with anybody else so, when they had a bad day at the office and didn't have any food themselves, nobody invited them round to have a bite. No sharing equaled no food equaled no kids. History may be written by the winners, but we're talking pre-pre-history here. If you're reading this blog post, it's because not all of your great-great-great-great-great-grandparents got chomped or starved or hit by a bus. The best predictor of who will not have children is those who don't have parents. Simply stated, those guys who didn't gather at the hearth and share food went the way of the Beta Max machine although, as I hope the preceding paragraphs have made clear, for entirely different reasons.

The take away for loving parents trying to bring up healthy kids in this toxic world where the dangers of large predators have been replaced with the threats of handheld devices is transparent: eat dinner with your kids.

Share you values with your children over veggie burgers if you like; model appropriate behaviors—not eating soup with your hands, for example—if you must, but whatever you do, gather round the hearth and have dinner with your kids.

Bonus points if the kids help shop for, prepare, and clean up after the meal. Extra credit if you have "sobre mesa", a leisurely conversation after eating. (No mention of homework, academic responsibilities, college applications, chores, or thank you notes allowed.)

Gathering at the hearth and sharing food is what made you into you. Gathering at the hearth and sharing food is what makes families into families.

73

My Scores are Too Small; My Nose is Too Big

"I just got my SATs back: 680 math which is terrible; 650 critical reading which is even worse. I just don't see myself getting into any of the schools I'm interested in. My counselor at school says that I don't have a chance at Brown, that there is no point in even applying. My counselor at school said the same thing about all the colleges I like. What's the point of even spending the money on the application fees if I won't get in? I'm taking four AP classes, studying between four and five hours every night, more on the weekends. I'm doing the best I can, but I just don't see anything good coming out of it long term. Yes, I have all As, but I got a B in AP History last year; all the other kids have better grades and harder classes. I'm the leading scorer on the soccer team, but we lost in the finals of the state tournament last year. I guess I'm lucky that my grandparents put away money for college and I can afford to go anywhere, but I'm not sure what good the money will do because I just know I won't get in. As soon as I saw my scores, I knew I had failed and failed miserably."

"Indeed, everything about me is completely and utterly wrong."

***

Every decent person who loves kids will take issue with each and every implication in the above soliloquy. This poor child is misguided and mistaken. Every decent person, counselor, and parent should help her internalize the following:

1) Her scores are fine. There are any number of wonderful colleges that would be pleased to admit a student with this profile: 1300 SATs; 3.8 unweighted GPA; soccer star; and full pay to boot. This child can most certainly go to college, almost any college.

2) Everyone—young women in particular—wishes she had done better on the SAT.

3) Studying four or five hours a day is plenty.

4) Applications cost about fifty bucks (The University of Florida is only $30; Tufts, outside Boston, is $70.) You wouldn't gamble fifty thousand dollars if you perceive that your odds of being admitted are bad, but fifty bucks isn't enough to get the family out of Chicken Kitchen at dinner time. There's no reason not to take a shot at one or two "reach" schools.

5) In <u>Reviving Ophelia: Saving the Selves of Adolescent Girls</u>, Mary Pipher points out that the White Rock mineral water girl in 1954 was 5'4" and weighed 140 pounds. Forty years later, the girl in the advert was 5' 10" and 110 pounds. Simple arithmetic extrapolation to 2014, gives us a 6' 1" tall girl who weighs 95 pounds, basically a stick with boobs. No one looks like this. No one healthy anyway. At this rate, by 2044, the girl would be 6' 7' and weigh 65 pounds, so my argument may not be perfect, but you take my point.

6) "In all the years, I've been a therapist," Pipher goes on to say, "I've yet to meet one girl who likes her body... They have been culturally conditioned to hate their bodies, which are after all themselves." Isn't the metaphor for SATs, which the girls accept as a proxy for their *minds*, just as cogent? The girls look in the cognitive mirror and, no matter what they see, they are disappointed and dissatisfied. In all the years I've been counseling, I've never met a girl who liked her scores.

7) The science of understanding and treating girls who self-harm is still in its infancy. Even the best mental health professionals aren't in clear agreement on where eating disorders or cutting behaviors come from or how to help the girls who suffer with these life-threatening maladies. But wouldn't you guess that a girl who hates herself is more likely to cut herself? On the other hand, wouldn't you guess that a girl who likes her body and likes her scores would be less likely to be promiscuous, throw up after meals, ingest ransom drugs, run away from home, and engage in other risky behaviors?

My gentle advice this week for loving parents is simple: love your kids for who they are. Not for what they look like. Not for what they got on their SATs.

Because, really, how are you going to find clothes for a 6' 7" daughter who weighs 65 pounds?

74

Can't We Agree to Agree?

Over breakfast recently, I mentioned in an overtly casually, pass the toast, sort of tone that I needed to travel to Northern Virginia to look at boarding schools.

"Where's the marathon?" my long-suffering wife responded instantly.

"I'm sure I don't know what you're talking about," I replied. "Ethical independent consultants have to consistently update their knowledge of traditional boarding schools around the country. A colleague of mine who was the director of admissions at one of my favorite New Hampshire schools recently became the head of a school in Virginia and I feel a responsibility to my clients to..."

"Where's the marathon?" Patti repeated in the same steely voice that has caused many a recalcitrant fifth grader on the playground to P-U-T T-H-A-T R-O-C-K D-O-W-N R-I-G-H-T N-O-W.

"What in the world makes you think that there's a marathon this time of year in Northern Virginia? Sometimes, I honestly just can't figure out how you get ideas in your head."

Patti was silent, but gave me "the look."

Clearly beaten, I fessed up: "It's the marathon of the Potomac," I admitted. That the packet pickup for the race is actually in D.C. rather than in Northern Virginia scored me no husband points whatsoever; I decided that "right now" would be an exceptionally propitious time to clear out those palm fronds and attend to a number of other tasks calling to me from the back yard.

In short, Patti saw straight through me. Were my forehead made of glass, she could not have been more accurate about my intention. I frequently plan my business travel to correspond with local races and she knows it. Some people like to play golf courses around the country; I like to see what the locals are doing at 26.2. Heck, traveling to the 48 contiguous states to check out indigenous meth labs would be worse.

But the point is that family members—your kids in particular—don't have to channel the Amazing Kreskin to know your opinion on matters ranging from studying to housework to promiscuity to underage drinking. They know what you think. The $64,000 question involves how to help our kids come to agree that our point of view involving sober attention to academics should take precedence over the prevailing opinion in our culture—that "fat, drunk, and stupid is [the] way to go through life."

Imagine, if you would, just how violently unpleasant it would be if you were forced to listen to political, social, or religious views in direct contrast to those which you hold dear. Perhaps you don't have to think back any further than a recent trip to an airport waiting room or your dentist's office. Pretty miserable, huh? Those talking heads pontificating endlessly about how the president is right (or wrong), the course we should follow in the middle east (or not), and how our immigration policy in the American Southwest is correct (or isn't.) Maddening, no? (Note to professionals, airports, and gas stations: turn the screens off. Please. We all have hand helds and, unlike when we're trapped at your place, we are allowed to change the channel or-gasp!—turn the thing off.)

You already know what those crackpots think. Their views are ubiquitous. The REASON you don't invite opinionated Republicans (or Democrats), Sunnis (or Shias), non-runners (or runners) to breakfast is that they are they don't agree with you. People with disparate points of view are welcome to engage in informed discussion at the evening meal, but please, not at breakfast.

If your kids are living in a home where they are constantly subjected to a barrage of views that contradict their own experience, they are likely to shut out their parents. And who could blame them? Thumper's advice applies to your children as much as to animated animals.

Or stated more succinctly: What makes you think that telling your son to do his homework for the one hundred and first time is going to make all the difference?

75

Change the Record

Where does negative self-talk come from? We've all gotten the same memo. You know the one I mean, the one that says: "You can't do it; you're not good enough." Where could a message this debilitating possibly come from?

A man whom I respected spoke over the years of how his mom never cuddled him or spoke the words, "I love you." He explained that in previous generations when times were tough (and times were pretty much always tough) there was a cultural meme: "Bad fortune and ruin will descend on the family who expresses affection or positive regard for its offspring." A vengeful and wrathful deity will smite those who articulate love for a child. Although plagues of locusts resulting from the utterance of affectionate words are hard to verify, this man became a successful academic. Admittedly, his life was an unending series of sadness—dissatisfaction, divorce, depression and ultimately suicide. But in fairness he was not, to my knowledge, overrun with bugs.

"You're all worthless and weak; now drop and give me twenty" didn't inspire the recruits and it doesn't resonate with your children either. "You're no good" gets internalized and repeated throughout the life cycle. "You're not loved" is the song that gets stuck in your head, the gift that keeps on giving, the tape without an off switch.

Could these endlessly repeated messages come from parents who communicate to their children that they are not loved for who they are? Who could possibly measure up to such a standard? "You are loved for what you do not for who you are" is a forever receding and ultimately unreachable finish line. The landmines along this psychic road to nowhere are ubiquitous.

Consider Jon Von Neumann, arguably the greatest mathematician of the 20th century. Von Neumann was a human computer. Seriously. He could multiply four digit numbers together in his head. And that "parlor trick" was the least of it. He worked on the Manhattan Project, was at the Institute of Advanced Studies, invented game theory, a whole new branch of mathematics. Yet, asked about his accomplishments late in life he is believed to have said, "I could have done more."

He could have done more? He helped invent nuclear weapons for goodness sake. Where does that leave your kids, presumably of significantly less innate ability and with fewer PhDs scattered about? We're talking about *major* science fair project here.

I know what you're thinking: "If I accept my children for who they are, they'll never do anything; they'll just sit around smelling the lotus blossoms. Motivation to achieve comes from being psychically uncomfortable. Human nature tends toward the slothful. If I don't yell at my kids, they won't do their homework."

I'm going to call this view of children, the "Gee, for a fat girl, you don't sweat much" school of parenting. And there's something else this "I only love my kids when they do what I want" paradigm reminds me of. The world's oldest profession involves similar transactions. All you have done is replace cash payments with affection.

I would not presume to pretend to have any insight into what the tape playing in Bruce Springsteen's mind says, but it is my understanding that the only time he can tune out the clutter is when he is performing. Apparently being carried aloft by adoring fans, body surfing along the outstretched arms of devoted aficionados any one of whom would gladly take a bullet for him, is the only way he knows to shut down the negative self-talk.

Make no mistake, I am in favor of rock in general and Bruce in particular, but what about the rest of us, those for whom a stadium replete with 70,000 screaming enthusiasts is unlikely (or as my offspring remind me: "Dad, when you play guitar, isn't that child abuse?")

How do we diminish mind chatter? How do we turn off or at least turn down the broken record? "You're not measuring up; you need to do more; you're not okay the way you are."

I don't know why people self-medicate. Why would an otherwise healthy individual drink enough alcohol so that he has diarrhea the next day after having barfed repeatedly the night before? I imagine there are as many reasons to drink to excess as there are brands of potato based spirits. Could a diminished sense of self be one of those reasons?

Woman at Fancy Dinner Party: Sir, if you were my husband, I would give you poison.

Winston Churchill: Madam, if you were my wife, I would drink it.

If you are listening to "you're not good enough" often enough, it's enough to drive you to drink.

Self-esteem doesn't result from being told how wonderful your kids perform. Self-esteem comes from being valued just for being who you are. Fast forward to adulthood: "I want to marry you because you have money." "I will love you forever because you have blonde hair." These relationships are doomed when economics and hair color change. Bruce Springsteen and Gary U.S. Bonds got it right:

"When your hair turns to silver,
I'll still call you, Delta Flower,
Pretty Blon, I'll still love you,
And I will wait for you."

I love you for who you are, not for what you look like or what your 1040 says is a blueprint for loving relationships of all kinds. Like lovers, parents must ultimately and at the deepest level communicate to their children unconditional positive regard. "You're okay just as you are" is a better record to imprint rather than the one about how you're no good. The loving message doesn't need to be drowned out with either fermented potatoes or screaming fans.

76

Salt

A new client introduced me to his daughter yesterday. Anna had been acting out at home, refusing to do assigned worksheets, not listening to her parents, and being as disrespectful as an adorable, gap-toothed eight-year-old child could be. "What can we do to get her to obey?" "How can we help her to be compliant?" "Why won't she do what we tell her?"

After listening patiently for an hour to what went on in the home of this well-meaning, highly educated, successful young couple, I formulated an answer: "The first thing you need to do," I began, "is to stop beating her with a belt."

"It's true, she is angelically well behaved at school" mom said. "The only time she is defiant and oppositional is at home."

I pointed out, as gently as I could, that at school no one hits her with an accessory meant to hold up clothes, not terrorize children. Being hit may produce temporary compliance but it also instills fear. Kids who are hit learn to hit. Their feelings of helplessness and frustration are seldom resolved in a healthy way. The word most often associated with "spanking" is "abuse."

If you, gentle reader, are sagaciously nodding your head, thinking "of course, we know better," I commend you. But before you break your arm patting yourself on the back, let me ask if there are any tools in your parenting shed used to enforce compliance and obedience rather than cooperation and love. Do you ever model fear rather than respect? Is sarcasm the moral equivalent of smacking in your home?

Home A: Please pass the salt.

Home B: What the matter? Are the f***ing salt pickers on strike?

***

Garrison Keillor got it right when he talked about taking both Prozac and Viagra. "But if either one worked, I wouldn't need the other." Similarly, if your home is filled with love, connection, fun, and attunement, you won't worry about compliance home or wanting to smack your kids.

What are other covert forms of mild abuse? What about forcing a "non-mathy" child to keep taking math year after year? Don't misunderstand. You know how much I love math. I enjoy math problems so much that I frequently spend my down time working on recreational math problems. I would rather work on a good math problem or logic puzzle than sit in a hot tub with Sofia Vergara. (Not that I am waiting by the phone for her call, mind you.) Email me and I'll send you links to sites filled with problems of every level and description that will keep you entertained for decades. I wish everyone who is capable would take math and more math, work hard and enjoy.

But for the kid who is never going to "get" calculus, shouldn't she be left alone to pursue her other abilities and passions at some point?

Sure, parents can force their kids to do stuff including calculus. With excessive force or sufficient incentives, compliance can be temporarily achieved and schedules maintained. But wouldn't you rather have someone who respects, admires, and loves you help you with the dishes rather than a recalcitrant employee grudgingly agreeing to do another vacuous worksheet?

"Being there" for your kids doesn't end when they are out of diapers and sleeping through the night in their own beds. Meeting the needs of your children continues right up until they pick out your nursing home.

And speaking of the time when the balance of decision making authority shifts to the next generation, wouldn't you rather that the person making the determination about whether or not to take you off life support is not someone whom you used to hit with a belt?

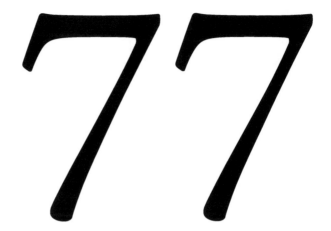

Where you Sit Determines What you See

A respected colleague makes the case for allowing kids to play video games. Not only do they enhance hand-eye coordination, but gaming is also the new form of reading, he suggests. Decrying video games because some are a waste of time is equivalent to throwing out all novels because Sweet Valley High is badly written. Good games are interactive and endlessly fascinating. Good games are eating the lunch of novels and other forms of fiction. The alternative to a good graphic game isn't <u>The Scarlett Letter</u> or <u>Moby Dick</u>. Kids read graphic novels on-line rather than reading books. Hours spent gaming may not be hours spent studying or developing a plan to end homelessness in your community, but time spent on programming is not hours spent taking drugs or mugging old ladies either. Gaming allows hard working productive students to relax.

And attempting to ban gaming in 2014 will be as productive as trying to get rid of alcohol a century earlier. Restrictions won't be effective; games are here to stay.

Good arguments surely, but from my chair the view is harshly different: I only see kids whose lives are spinning out of control as a result of unhealthy relationships with screens of all kinds. "If you take away my game, I'll kill myself" said one unhappy child in my office recently. Another young man, already in treatment, threw his iPad across the room; had his aim been better, a fellow student would have been bruised. My clients are playing video games when they should be studying, when they should be learning social skills by interacting with other humans. My kids are playing video games when they should be eating.

There is no argument to be made against an adult having a glass of wine of a weekend evening. Those who drink to feel good harm no one.

But those who drink so that they don't feel bad are another story. There's no end to the misery—as anyone with an alcoholic or drug addicted family member can attest.

I can't argue for prohibition. I can argue for making a distinction between those who can play games safely and those who can't. A student who performs in school and fulfills his responsibilities to himself and his family can play video games. A student who stays in his basement sucking on screens nine hours a day, not so much.

The trick of course is determining who is a social gamer and who has an addiction spiraling out of control. Of a roomful of college kids drinking beer on a Saturday night, most will grow up to have a healthy relationship with alcohol, a few will be problem drinkers for the rest of their lives, a smaller number will die as a direct consequence of their alcohol consumption.

What are loving parents to do? Parents must provide attractive alternatives to the siren song of screens. Just as few children will choose a healthy meal when there are alternatives that open the door for diabetes (chips, ice cream, and chocolate frosted sugar bombs trump vegetable lasagna any day) parents have to fill their homes with Parcheesi games and peers with whom to play.

"But all the families in our neighborhood allow their kids to play video games as much as they like." Nah. That's exactly what they're saying about you. If your house is the one without screens, you'll find the kids who want to hang out there. Playing dress up and playing outside are easily acquired tasted.

You wouldn't let your ten-year smoke cigarettes or drink beer. Why would you expose her to screens to which she can easily become addicted?

"But she has to have a healthy relationship with technology. She has to use the Internet for research in school and email for communication." Of course. But she doesn't have to spend three hours a day on Facebook while she's supposed to be reading, studying or thinking. And she certainly doesn't have to be playing "Shoot, Shoot, Shoot, Blood, Blood, Blood, Kill, Kill, Kill" when she's supposed to be living her life.

You heard it here first.

78

I am Spartacus

The glorious slave rebellion has been thoroughly and horribly defeated. The Roman conquerors personified by the corrupt senator Marcus Licinius Crassus (impeccably portrayed by Laurence Olivier) want to send a message to future generations of slaves that will last a thousand years. The Romans intend to nail the leader of the rebellion, Spartacus, (Kirk Douglas in his finest role,) to two pieces of wood where he will die an excruciatingly prolonged and painful death. The only problem for the triumphant Romans is that they don't know which of the thousands of subjugated warriors is the leader.

If the conquered army will give up Douglas, each man will be rewarded with a quick and painless end. Only Spartacus will die in agony on the cross. If, on the other hand, the enslaved and defeated men remain silent, each and every one of them will also die horribly.

Spartacus is ready to identify himself. There is no reason for everyone to be tortured to death. Spartacus has led the doomed uprising from the beginning and accepts responsibility. But before he can stand up and declare who he is, Antoninus (Tony Randall)—in what is arguably the greatest scene in the history of celluloid—stands up and affirms, "I am Spartacus."

As Douglas looks on in disbelief, another slave stands up and shouts, "I am Spartacus." And another. And another. And another.

To the last man, the warrior slaves are willing to die for their cause, for their community, for their shared vision of a world where they would not be slaves.

***

Yesterday an acquaintance whom I had not seen in some years asked me about my children. (Stay with me here; I'll make my point about the movie in a paragraphs or two.) As it happens, my kids are fine. All four of them are where they need to be. None of my kids is in the emergency room. Everything good here.

So I should just answer my friend's polite inquiry with a litany of how wonderful my kids are, right? What could possibly be the harm of recounting their recent successes, maybe even bragging a little? After all, aren't the accomplishments of my wonderful children a reflection of what a good parent I am?

But what if my kids weren't okay?

What if one of my kids had just dropped out of college and was in a psychiatric hospital for severe depression? What if one of my kids were in treatment for a life-threatening eating disorder? What if one of my beloved children were in jail for a big drug deal gone bad?

Attorneys teach us not to ask questions to which we don't know the answers. Shouldn't we also hesitate to ask questions to which we don't <u>want</u> to know the answers?

I have friends whose kids aren't doing well. You do also. Shouldn't we protect the privacy of these good folks and allow them to walk their difficult path in peace? Don't they have enough to worry about with a kid in the hospital or a child in jail without having to deal with "How're your kids?" all day long?

I'm not telling you not to be proud of your kids. I am just suggesting that you don't have to tell everybody about it. I'm not saying my old friend wasn't just trying to be polite. I'm just saying that I'm sticking up for families whose kids aren't doing well at present.

"Everybody is fine" and "We're all good, thanks for asking" are noncommittal answers that everyone can make whether our kids were just graduated from college with a complex double major or, on the other hand, flunked out of school and are desperately unemployed.

By not bragging about your kids when they are doing well, you become part of a broader community where children are valued for who they are rather than what they do. In communities where all children are appreciated, we get more college graduates and fewer inmates. By saying, "The kids are all right" rather than disclosing your children's SAT scores, you are, in a very real sense, standing up and saying "I am Spartacus."

I'm not sure it gets any better than that.

79

And the One that Mother Gives You

I am not a medical professional nor do I play one on TV. I do not have a degree in psychiatry. Although I am a frequent blood donor, I still look away when the needle goes in my arm and I get queasy when my wife watches ER reruns. In short, my medical advice should be considered with a mound of salt and is only marginally better than my insights into the stock market which can be summarized as: "Keep investing till it's gone." With those caveats firmly in place, here's my thought: it's entirely likely that your child is over-medicated.

At the very least, she is likely on the wrong meds and the wrong path.

I have seen the good that psycho-stimulants can do. For motivated students who choose to focus on their studies but are distracted by attentional issues, adderall, vivance, stytera and the like can be helpful. But for students who don't WANT to attend to memorizing the capitals of the 50 states (yes, this vacuous curriculum is still taught in the age of information) these prescriptions are likely to have the following problems.

1)   There's a pill for that.

Kids who internalize the lesson that pills are okay are more likely to take non-prescription, recreational, life-destroying, deadly drugs wouldn't you think? Pills for attention, pills for sleep, pills to wake up, pills to remind you to take your other pills, pills to make you feel good, pills to make you not feel bad.

2)   There's another pill for that.

When the pills for attention don't work and the kid is still boinging across the classroom like Speedy Gonzalez on fast forward, frantic parents try SSRIs to cure bi-polarity which doesn't work because the kid wasn't bi-polar to begin with so the desperate parents move on to atypical anti-psychotics followed by mood stabilizers. That's a lot of pills for a kid who was just basically energetic and had trouble sitting still and attending to vacuous, mind-numbing curriculum. (Do YOU know the capital of Vermont? Neither do I.)

3)   Decreased effectiveness over time

Remember in <u>Flowers for Algernon</u> when the cognitively impaired protagonist, after becoming the smartest guy who ever lived, starts to lose his ability and slide back down to where he was, once again unable to read or write well or understand social cues? There is a growing body of research to suggest that psycho-stimulants help effect gains for about three years and then the kids are no better than where they were before they started "using." This result is bad news for the pharmaceutical companies and worse news for a generation of drugged adolescents.

So what's the answer?

Surely, "go out and play" isn't all there is to this issue although I would agree that "a tired dog is a good dog." It's developmentally inappropriate for elementary school children to sit at desks all day and then be expected to produce worksheets all night. There is something to be said for lying on your back on a warm afternoon trying to figure out what the clouds look like and then rolling down the hill in a heap. Whenever I hear about a kid who won't sit still and "doesn't attend" to curriculum and "refuses" to pay attention in the classroom and distains homework and "won't" go to bed at a reasonable hour, I think about taking said kid on a four-day/three-night hiking and camping trip 40 miles from the nearest electrical outlet or bathroom. Show me a kid walking through a slot canyon in Utah in river water up to his knees for six hours a day and I'll show you a kid who is beyond eager to fall asleep before you can say, "Did anyone remember to tie the backpacks up in a tree so the bears don't get them like they did that time year before last?" I'll also show you a kid who will eat anything that doesn't move and some things that do. I don't know whether or not there are atheists in foxholes, but I'm thoroughly convinced there are no fussy eaters on camping trips. And I see kids labeled as ADHD and heavily medicated in the city who are able to "attend" just fine to the more subtle cues of functioning in the outdoors.

In Dungeons and Dragons, players get to pick attributes including strength, speed, agility, and emotional stability for their characters. (Okay, I made up the emotional stability part, but that would have been fun, don't you think?) So suppose you got to pick the features of your kid. Would you pick smart? Sure. Would you pick motivated? Of course. Would you pick successful? Why not?

But what if, like the ring of Sauron in The Lord of the Rings, there was a price to pay for having all those desirable traits?

The qualities smart and stressed don't HAVE to go together, but lately I don't see too many kids at the top of their class who got there effortlessly. Instead I see sleep deprived kids whose educations make no sense to them or to anybody else. I see unhappy kids. Loving parents might want to think about internalizing the following mantra: "I'd rather have a joyful, content, fun-loving, sober carpenter's assistant than a highly successful, stressed-to-the-point-of-snapping, addicted, frenetic, miserable, thrice-divorced orthopedic surgeon.

Because as my grandmother often remarked, "You're a long time dead" and I remain convinced that there is no pill for that.

80

Hidden Agenda

Paul returns to the off-campus apartment he shares with Nick who is, once again, slouched over the couch watching skate-boarding videos on their big screen while playing "Call of Duty" on his iPad. Paul notices, beyond the pile of empty pizza boxes and discarded beer cans, a three-foot pile of dirty dishes in the sink. Paul addresses his roommate as follows:

"I am sick and tired of doing your dishes, Nick. You are such a slob. When we decided to get this place, you said you would be responsible for doing half the dishes, but you never do any dishes. Your dirty dishes are going to attract roaches and rats. Look at all these disgusting dishes. I am so over your not doing any dishes."

Press "pause" on the DVR recording of this interaction between these two 19-year-olds for a moment and answer one straight-forward question: What does Nick "hear"? What has Paul communicated? What is the emotion that Paul has conveyed? What is Paul's agenda?

If you said, "Paul is angry" or "Paul is feeling frustrated," I agree.

How will Nick respond? My guess is that he will become defensive and point out that Paul never vacuums like he promised he would or that most of the dirty dishes are, in actuality, Paul's. Paul might then mention that if Nick would pick up the darn beer cans that maybe there would be room to run the vacuum. Nick might mention a borrowed jersey that wasn't returned. The conversation may escalate to include accusations about past girlfriends, disappointments, and broken promises. The only guarantee in this rabbit hole scenario is that the dishes—remember the dishes?—will not get done.

Were Paul, on the other hand, to walk in, observe the same pile of dishes and blaring skateboarding videos, and say, "Hi, Nick. If you'll wash the dishes, I'll dry them and then we can go down to the campus cafeteria and see if there's anybody who wants to play basketball", then Nick is likely to say, "Sure. Sounds good." Paul's agenda is one of cooperation. The dishes will get done.

In the scenario when Paul got overwhelmed with anger, he used the word "dishes" half a dozen times, but Nick never heard anything about dishes. Nick just heard frustration. On the other hand, when Paul communicated "let's get the job done," he only used the word "dishes" once.

Exactly the same situation; completely different outcomes.

What is your agenda when you help your fifth grade child with his homework? What is your child "hearing" you communicate?

1) We're all in this together; I'm happy to help.

Or

The world is an uncertain, horrible place and my anxiety about the future is out of control.

Will your child understand that?

2) In this family we help each other

Or

You are not okay. Unless you do these worksheets, you will be an even bigger loser than you already are.

Will your child come to acknowledge that?

3) Learning is important to me and it gives me great joy to convey that value to you. I have always loved reading and I hope my beloved child will as well.

Or

You must do what your teacher tells you. Even though these assignments are vacuous and you're not learning anything other than blind obedience to vapid authority.

Of course a lot of what your child hears when you sit down to help him with his homework is dependent on what your relationship has been to that point. If your child sees you as "that's the person I want to be like when I grow up," help with homework may be seen as a welcome boon and a chance to hang out and learn. If, to the contrary, your child sees you as "that person who is always telling me to do things, who doesn't like me the way I am, who keeps telling me I'm no good," the interaction may be significantly less productive and pleasant.

If I wanted to convey to you, gentle reader, an agenda of respect and affection as well as an agenda of helping you and your child connect in the most meaningful and agreeable way, I might recommend a "no homework zone" on Saturday afternoon during which you sit on the couch with your child and re-read <u>Harry Potter and the Prisoner of Azkaban</u>. The hidden agenda of "my kid and I love hanging out together on a rainy weekend afternoon and taking an exquisite mental bubble bath of imagination and language" in not one that your child is likely to misinterpret.

81

What is a Swimmer's Dream?

I am determined to seduce and marry Veronica Lake. Hear me out. She is beautiful, a movie star, and has a lot of money. I just know our lives together will be exquisite. Admittedly, she doesn't know I'm alive nor is she aware of my undying passion or my plan to be with her forever. But I know just what to do. I have been working on this strategy for the last four years and I am thoroughly convinced that it will work. I have found out the last known address for Veronica, somewhere in Beverly Hills. Although there is an eight-foot wall around the property, I have spent the last several semesters writing poetry and throwing the poems over the wall. I just feel it in my heart that she is reading and appreciating them. I also serenade her by walking back and forth along the sidewalk in front of her house singing love songs that I have written. No, I don't particularly like writing poetry nor do I have an ear or appreciation for music, but I am willing to do anything so that Veronica will notice me, fall in love with me, and marry me.

Some people have had the unmitigated temerity to suggest that Veronica and I will not be a good match, that we are ill suited for one another. These people are just jealous fools. For example, some stupid actor, Joel McCrea, refused to be in another film with her because he said, "Life's too short for two films with Veronica Lake." And this author guy, Raymond Chandler, referred to her as "Moronica Lake." So, okay, you can't please everybody. As far as the fact that she's been married four times, well, people make mistakes. But she's so pretty. I just know we would be happy. I know that after her movie career deteriorated she lived in cheap hotels and was frequently arrested for public drunkenness, but, like I said, you can't have everything.

I am a determined guy; I always get what I want. (And when I don't, I'm not that much fun to be around.) I don't let myself get confused by the facts. I am convinced that Veronica will be impressed if I learn to play the bouzouki so I have been practicing four hours a day, all the time I can spare when I'm not writing poetry for Veronica or walking back and forth outside the address I have for where I think she lives.

***

Change "Veronica Lake" in the monologue above to "admission to a 'top' college" and you have the sad lives or many current high school students. Rather than doing what gives them pleasure, they hurl themselves down the lonely road to nowhere hoping to impress unseen admissions officers at colleges about which they know nothing. Rather than taking courses they would enjoy and from which they would learn, they blindly follow dictums about what course selection and extra-curriculars will "get them in."

Wouldn't this child's interests be better served by engaging in those activities in which he might excel? Shouldn't he direct his energy toward that which he enjoys rather than pursuing only that which he thinks Veronica will value? By his own admission, he doesn't like playing guitar or writing poetry and nobody likes walking back and forth in front of an empty home, yet nothing will dissuade our "Princeton or Perish" young man from "pursuing his dream," "overcoming adversity," and "achieving his goal." (Not that there's anything wrong with Princeton, mind you, but not everyone gets in.) And what about when he learns that Veronica Lake is dead? (According to Wikipedia, the source from which I got all the facts above, Lake died in 1973.) No matter how inappropriate the match, out applicant still won't give up. Wouldn't he better off following his passion, learning what he loves, and preparing himself to be successful wherever he ends up in college?

The take-away for loving parents is simple enough: encourage your children to have goals that make sense, goals that will bring them contentment—obsessing over schizophrenic, dead movie stars, no matter how beautiful, is probably not on this list.

82

Horrible, Horrible, Horrible

"That's horrible," Janet interrupted. "What's the point of having children if you're just going to send them away to boarding school?"

Lynn, who had been talking about attending boarding school as a child fell silent as Janet continued: "I would never send my kids to boarding school."

It was clear to me that Lynn's feelings were hurt. Indeed, it was obvious to everyone at the dinner party that Janet had made an error in judgment. Now that I reflect, it was obvious to everyone in Miami-Dade County that Janet had her foot solidly in her mouth. Had there been a recent immigrant from Mars who had been studying the culture of her nearest solar system neighbor for just under two weeks, the gaff would have been obvious to that newly-arrived creature as well. Frankly, I'm surprised that you didn't call me to discuss this rending of the social fabric when the shock waves of Janet's offensive remark hit your house and knocked that book on etiquette off your mantel piece.

Undeterred by the disruption in the moral composition of the universe, Janet blundered on: "I mean, do you love your kids or don't you? Boarding school? Why not just drop them off at an orphanage and be done with it?"

There was more of the same from Janet. "Why would anyone send their children to boarding school? Why? What is wrong with people?" But I have too much fondness for you, gentle reader, to subject you to another syllable. And fortunately for me, I was able to tune out by focusing on something more pleasant—having my body torn apart and devoured by wolves, for example.

Let's ignore, for the moment, the myriad of eventualities that may have allowed Lynn's parents to choose boarding school: maybe the family had a boarding school tradition stretching back generations; maybe Lynn had learning differences that could not be addressed by the schools in her town; maybe her parents were in poor health; maybe Lynn wanted to ride horses or take advantage of the rich texture of education and extra-curriculars that boarding schools offer. We'll never know that specifics because Janet's imperious interruption shut the door on my learning more about Lynn and her family.

I'm just an old math teacher so I want to enumerate the two possibilities here: Either Janet is right—it is always unequivocally wrong to allow a child to attend a boarding school—or she's wrong. If Janet is right, then it is horrible to point out the fact that Lynn's parents erred. On the other hand, if Janet is wrong, then it is stupid to make her ignorant outlook so loudly and violently known.

As my grandfather used to say, "When you wake up in the morning, you want to be able to shoot higher than either horrible or stupid."
I wish I knew who originally pointed out that opinions are like digestive systems in that everyone has one, but it is unlikely that anyone wants to hear about yours.

For parents, it is imperative to know when to keep our mouths shut. "More than you might think" is my first approximation in that our kids already know our opinions. Since our kids do as we do rather than as we say anyway, during carpool we might as well eavesdrop rather than pontificate. You never know what you might pick up.

You know those people who don't listen, who just wait for their turn to talk? Don't be one of them. Elevate your sights above either horrible or stupid.

83

Mine, Mine, Mine

You know the guy I'm talking about. If you have ever driven a car in Miami, you have seen this guy repeatedly. He is swerving in and out of traffic, changing lanes without using his turn signal. On a given day, rather than wait, he will abandon the main arteries, careen through residential neighborhoods, and drive across your front lawn. Ignoring stop signs in suburban enclaves is fine with this guy just so he doesn't get where he's going a minute later.

That his getting to work earlier means that someone else gets to work later neither occurs to nor concerns him. He fits right in with the "me, me, me" sensibilities of our time. Don't call him about volunteering; making a contribution to the community is not on his list. This is a man in a hurry.

If getting to work on time were a single elimination tournament, perhaps this self-centered driving could be overlooked. Many people have forgiven that psychotic, immoral, intimidating, cheating, creepy bully who absconded with all those bike race trophies. In athletics, as I am not the first to remark, somebody wins and somebody loses. In rush hour traffic, everybody could get to work on time IF our insensitive subject gets up ten minutes earlier and waits his turn instead of zipping along in the "right turn only" lane and cutting the line at the last minute.

His agenda, that he and his schedule are important and that you and your commitments are not, is clear.

Where is he going on Saturday morning, driving his Porsche 20 miles over the speed limit even though traffic is light? He is driving his daughter to the bouzouki competition 45 minutes across town because his daughter is applying to "top" colleges. Our Mario Andretti wannabe is firmly convinced that college admissions officers are clawing one another to attract the top bouzouki players.

The following actual facts regarding admissions to colleges make no impression on our guy:

Bouzouki competition victories notwithstanding, his daughter is not likely to be admitted to a "top" school.

Her life would be an unrelenting misery if she were.

Only a few years ago our guy was lurking in the parking lot "chatting" with teachers, wanting to make sure he understood how the captain of the cheer-leading squad was to be chosen. He just wanted to make sure that his daughter had every chance (read: every advantage) to get that position so that someone else's daughter would not.

Remember your outrage at hearing that the wife of the Shah of Iran took baths in fresh milk while the people in her country went hungry? Shouldn't you feel the same disdain for this guy, sucking up our shared resources?

Shouldn't we feel sorry for his bouzouki playing cheerleader daughter who knows at every level of her being that her father loves her more for where she will go to college than for who she is?

Will and Ariel Durant tell a story about Napoleon's mother: Napoleon's mother watched as hundreds of her son's soldiers carried box and box along the road toward her castle. Six men were required to carry each box because each box was filled with 20,000 gold coins. On each coin was stamped the image of her son, the ruler of the majority of the known world. As the boxes were stacked in room after room in the castle basement, as one of the greatest fortunes in history was amassed, Napoleon's mother is reputed to have said, "It's not enough."

Ten generations later, I get the feeling that Napoleon's mother is insisting that her daughter win the cheer-leading and bouzouki competitions and go to a "top college." I get the feeling that Napoleon's mother would also have been willing to leave skid marks as she careened across your front lawn.

84

The Un-safest Sex of All

Surely there are enough intrusions into the privacy of your bedroom without my asking yet another boundary crossing question. No reality TV for me, thank you very much. My own life—with which I can barely keep up—entertains me just nicely; I can't imagine trying to stay abreast of what somebody else is doing, thinking, or feeling on an uninhabited island or in New Jersey. But at the risk of intruding into your reality, here's a thought experiment: do you think the teenagers and young adults in your life have ever been physically intimate sober?

Stated even more inappropriately: do you think your kids have ever had sex when they weren't drunk or stoned?

If this question is too uncomfortable to think about, consider your next door neighbor's kid rather than your own. Or think about kids in a distant community, but the question remains: are sexually active kids having sex sober?

I'm going to argue that, for the majority of teens and young adults the answer is "No." I'm going to suggest that for many young folks, the only circumstance under which they have sex, especially with a new partner, is when they have been drinking alcohol or smoking pot.

Could they be conceptualizing the process as follows? I don't like the way I look; I'm embarrassed about my body. My whole life, every advert I see insists that I am simultaneously too tall, too short, too fat, too thin and that I smell bad. No way I'm going to live in this skin and in all my anxiety. If I'm drunk, it doesn't count. If I don't want to remember what I did, I can remember what I did any way I want.

Or like this? I have absorbed the message that I'm supposed to be an insensitive hunter without feelings or concerns, but I'm not sure that's who I am. I am going to deaden my feelings to three steps beyond numb so that I don't have to deal with any anxiety or recriminations. "After" I can just pretend nothing happened.

Sober sex, or what a researcher described as "eyes open" sex requires thought and thoughtfulness, communication and reciprocity, qualities not overly abundant in many marriages never mind youthful populations. A sober thought, "Maybe my partner would like this?" can be replaced by a fuzzy grope, "I might like that."

A goodly number of electrons were expended a couple months ago when the New York Times front page detailed the alleged rape of a young girl and the subsequent cover-up by campus police at Hobart and William Smith College. A similar incident at FSU got even bigger headlines although, if possible, an even smaller punishment for the alleged football star perpetrator.

Here is what I'm not going to do:

I'm not going to blame the victim. I'm not going to suggest that the young women were in any way at fault. They weren't provocative, they weren't "asking for it," they weren't "looking for trouble" by being at a fraternity party. They are blameless for the attacks.

These young women have suffered enough: from the vicious attacks during the incidents to the blatantly mishandled subsequent cover-ups. They—and

ozens more like them on campuses every year—don't need more
stigating from me.

Here is what I am going to do:

I am going to remind all my young people that the best way not to get in a bar fight is to not go into a bar. I'm going to point out to all young women that yes, you are entitled to go out and listen to music at the venue of your choice and yes, you should be safe on your campuses. But no, "Nothing good happens after midnight." The first way to avoid being the victim of a brutal crime by these thugs is not to be where they are. Yes, the bad guys are everywhere. But the bad guys are especially well represented at fraternity parties where one of them just happened to show up with 300 gallons of alcohol. My advice is NOT to be at these parties. There's nothing good going on at these frats at two in the morning on a Saturday night/Sunday morning. Nothing. Ever. (The beach cleanups and tutoring of economically distressed populations that fraternities use to justify their existences? These activities, if they happen at all, are not happening at two in the morning.) What do these young women expect, that they're going to meet a decent man with whom they are going to have a meaningful romantic tryst? Decent men are less likely to be doing Jello shots and barfing off the balcony.

I am in favor of taking back the streets and speaking truth to power. I am in favor of safe campuses where young women can walk innocently to their dorms after sipping a convivial glass of Chardonnay. I like to believe that the meek shall inherent the earth, but in the meantime, I am not mortgaging the farm to go all-in on the meek. While I'm waiting for the meek to start coming back in the late innings and win some games, I'm going to remember that the best way to get out of trouble is to stay out of trouble. My young women need to focus on finding some sober companions and finding some sober fun. If you want to have sex, do so when you're ready and when you're not totally schnockered. You also may want to consider choosing a partner whom you'd like to see again—conceivably when he's not wearing an orange jump suit.